T0195904

Sharing the Years

Sharing
the Years

Linda Lear Shofner

Book Cover Illustration by Weslie Shofner

authorHOUSE®

AuthorHouse™
1663 Liberty Drive
Bloomington, IN 47403
www.authorhouse.com
Phone: 1-800-839-8640

© 2014 Linda Lear Shofner. All rights reserved.

No part of this book may be reproduced, stored in a retrieval system, or transmitted by any means without the written permission of the author.

Published by AuthorHouse 10/08/2014

ISBN: 978-1-4969-4530-3 (sc)
ISBN: 978-1-4969-4529-7 (hc)
ISBN: 978-1-4969-4528-0 (e)

Library of Congress Control Number: 2014917905

Any people depicted in stock imagery provided by Thinkstock are models, and such images are being used for illustrative purposes only. Certain stock imagery © Thinkstock.

This book is printed on acid-free paper.

Because of the dynamic nature of the Internet, any web addresses or links contained in this book may have changed since publication and may no longer be valid. The views expressed in this work are solely those of the author and do not necessarily reflect the views of the publisher, and the publisher hereby disclaims any responsibility for them.

Acknowledgements

Special thanks are in order to all who were kind enough to read my first book, *Shared Years*, and ask, "When is the sequel going to be ready?" That gave me the encouragement to go on and write *Sharing the Years.* I hope you enjoy this book as much as you enjoyed *Shared Years.*

Again, I must thank my proofreaders, my good friend, Darlene and my ever diligent and helpful niece, Nona. They gave me unending assistance with the first book, with book launch parties for it, and with proofing this one. Again, all you English majors out there, put your red pens away, and try to get lost in the story line. You will, I am sure, as we did, find mistakes even after all the numerous reviews that we did. My ninety-seven year-old mother found the biggest mistake in the last book near the end when I used Chris' name where I should have used Tom's. She will not be assisting me this time as we lost Mama in June of this year. You will see many of her qualities in Katie, the grandmother, who appears in both books.

The covers for both of these books are the work of my son, Weslie. Many thanks to him. I would not want anyone else doing my book covers. He understands what I want and creates better things than I would ever have imagined. Keep creating, Wes. It is what you do best.

Thanks to Author House for being so patient in waiting for this second book. To all of you in that organization, know that I am grateful for the assistance that you provided.

Thanks to Mrs. Lillian Kazee for the use of her recipe, not only in this book, but for all the many times I have used it to glorious reviews. I highly recommend that all you cooks out there try it.

Last, thanks to J. E., my husband, for listening to me and laughing with me at all the trials one goes through when trying to publish a book. An amateur, I am, but it has been fun and challenging.

Kaye thought for sure the car would slip off the road before she could make it back safely to Tom. Ice storms in Kentucky weren't the norm, but after being stranded for nearly three days in Lexington, she had learned a great deal about survival. She had to laugh at that thought. She'd been able to make her way to a motel and keep reasonably warm, even when the electrical power in the immediate area had failed. Plus, there was plenty of food in the restaurant attached to the motel. She had not gone hungry or been in any sort of life threatening danger.

She had learned, however, that she needed to be better prepared in cases of bad weather like she had just experienced. She had made notes to put warm coveralls in her trunk along with a blanket, and a collapsible shovel in case she ever had to dig her car out of a snow bank. In addition, she had decided she would buy some kitty litter to put under her tires to give her traction. She'd buy enough litter to get out of a situation where her car was stuck or spinning and going nowhere on ice or snow. She would survive the next ice and snowstorm a little better than she had this one. She definitely knew that she would pay more attention to weather forecasts in the future. She did not want to be stuck out in weather as unprepared as she had been this time, not ever again.

Survive, indeed! She had come through this disaster quite well compared to many people across the state that had been nowhere nearly as lucky. Shelters throughout the state had served as a refuge, and were still being used by people in places where the power was yet to be restored. She had received a phone call from her friend, Stacy, saying that the school where they worked was open for people to use.

Kaye wondered if they would return from the Christmas break on the scheduled date, or would that be delayed because of needing the school for a shelter. She also wondered, *How are they feeding all those people? Maybe they brought in the lunchroom staff using Humvees or 4-wheel drives.* Stacy told her the Principal was staying at the school twenty-four/seven and actually had one of the emergency cots in his office using it to sleep.

Kaye could just see him guarding the place. Thinking about all that could be stolen from a school in a time like that, was something that she was glad was his job and not hers.

Now, if she could just keep this darn car on the road until she could get to Tom, she might never leave him again. The expressways were clear and traffic was moving on them. The side roads, however, weren't as passable. Tom and some neighbors had worked with a local crew to clear the roads in their area, and the temperatures had allowed some of the ice to melt in some places. But, she was several miles away from Tom's and the area where she was driving was not as clear. There were areas, sheltered from the sun, where black ice was still a big problem.

Flashing red lights from the ambulance coming up behind her caused her to inhale deeply. She had nowhere to go. She couldn't pull over. The snow along the road was too deep. She stepped on her brakes *very slowly* to let the ambulance driver pass.

As she rounded the next curve she could see red and blue lights ahead. She eased on her brakes and slowly came to a complete stop without sliding. An officer was standing in the road and she said a small prayer while she was waiting for directions from him. The accident looked pretty serious. The officer walked back to her car and she recognized him as the local DARE Officer that serviced her school.

"Hello, Miss Mason. What on earth are you doing out on these roads? It isn't safe."

"Well, Officer Howell, I went shopping in Lexington before this ice storm hit and got stranded there. I'm trying to get home."

"Don't you live with your grandparents? This isn't the road to their place."

"Yes, I'm living with them now, but I was actually trying to get to Tom Scott's place."

"Oh, yes. I heard about your engagement. Have you two set a date yet?" *Wow! That was fast!* Kaye thought, *How had this officer already heard about her engagement?* Then she thought, *Small town news travels fast.*

"No, not yet."

They placed a patient in the ambulance and closed the doors on a frantic team of EMS workers. Kaye listened as the screaming of the siren sliced through the cold air sending shivers over her.

"That person must be hurt pretty badly."

"Yes, ma'am, but not as badly as the other one. I'm afraid you're gonna be stuck here a few minutes, Miss Mason. The county coroner is on her way."

"Oh, gee! Someone's been killed?"

"Yes, I'm afraid so. It's an older couple—out of state license. Not sure why they were out here on this road. Might have been lost."

Kaye watched as they cleared the scene thinking how swiftly life could be taken from you. She called her grandmother to tell her she was on her way to Tom's so Grandma Katie wouldn't be worried, and she certainly didn't want her grandfather being concerned, especially not after his triple by-pass. She explained about the wreck and said she'd call as soon as she was safe at Tom's.

Tom was watching out the window thinking Kaye was way past due, and then the telephone rang. He was so glad to hear Kaye's voice on the other end. He wanted to reach through those telephone lines and touch her, just to have tangible evidence that she was okay.

She explained why she was delayed and he asked if the accident victims were local folks. She told him the license plates were from out of state, so she didn't think the people were local. Then she explained that she was only about fifteen miles away and should be with him soon.

Tom returned to the window. At the moment, fifteen miles seemed more like a thousand. How in the world had he fallen so deeply in love? It was scary. A love this strong carried so many possibilities with it. One was losing the person you loved. Tom didn't even want to think about that. It could hurt in an incredibly deep way.

Damn, Tom! Get away from the negative thoughts! he commanded himself. *Kaye is on her way to you.*

Another possibility was to spend a lifetime like Kaye's parents and grandparents had, building a life together that meant something. That was something that Tom really wanted.

He remembered Kaye's phone calls from Lexington. She hadn't told him she was going. Then she explained that she was going to the gynecologist she used while she attended the University of Kentucky to get her birth control pills renewed. She didn't want to use the local pharmacy just yet. She didn't want to add any more fuel to the rumors that were already spreading around their small community about her and Tom.

Kaye had gotten those pills the first time to have protection from pregnancy when she had decided to have a sexual relationship with the law student she was dating. That relationship went sour on her before they became really intimate, however, and Tom had wound up falling in love with a girl who had not had actual sex with another man—a virgin.

When Tom found out that Kaye had not slept with anyone, it nearly scared him to death. She was the granddaughter of the man he had just made a big crop leasing deal with. He knew better than to mess around with Roth Mason's granddaughter. You just didn't mess with a man like Roth.

Damn it! Is that little compact car ever going to show up?
Then Tom's worried expression suddenly relaxed. She had finally
arrived and they were going to set that wedding date as soon as he
could get it to happen.

He didn't like the jealous feeling he had when Kaye called
him from the motel in Lexington two days ago to tell him that
her former law-student boyfriend was stranded at the same motel.
How coincidental could that be? he wondered. He had to fight the
green-eyed monster of jealously, but he knew that he'd have to
learn to trust, and Kaye had told him about it. She could have
kept it a secret. *Pretty, smart, and honest, too—what more could a
man want?* he told himself, feeling pretty fortunate to be able to
have a relationship with a woman like Kaye Mason.

Kaye could see Tom's house and she felt such a relaxed
feeling of contentment. It would soon be the house they would
share. She almost wanted to throw the birth control pills out the
window. She could see a couple of kids running around in that
yard building snowmen, swinging in a swing set, making mud
pies, getting skinned knees and asking for Band-Aids; doing all
the things kids do.

Tom was at the car before she could get it parked. He had
her in a bear hug as soon as she stood up.

Simultaneously they said, "We have to set that wedding
date!" Both of them laughed and they kissed, hoping the feeling
would never end.

Kaye grabbed two bags from the backseat. One held a cell
phone she bought for Tom while she was in Lexington. She had
called him and told him she was buying it because she always
wanted to be connected to him. The other bag contained a change
of clothes she had stopped and purchased at Wal-Mart on the way
home from Lexington. She had only meant to drive to Lexington
for the day. Anticipating that she'd be stuck there, for three days, in
the same clothes, was not something for which she had prepared.

She had washed undies in the sink at the motel and had been able to shower, but she had been in her outer clothing way too long.

"Tom, I need a bath and I bought a change of clothes. I hope I don't smell too bad."

"You smell great. The electricity is still not on out here, but I have some hot water in the old wood cook stove of my grandmother's that's still in the kitchen. Boy! Am I glad I didn't get rid of that thing! It's been a life saver through this ice storm."

"I'm glad you didn't get rid of it, too, and we're going to keep it."

"It has a water reservoir on the side and I have it full of water. The kitchen is warm from the heat coming from the stove. You can take a pan bath in there. Hey, can I watch?"

"Stop it, Tom! I've been uncomfortable enough these past few days without having to take a bath in front of someone."

"I don't want to make you uncomfortable. I just want to watch." Kaye didn't answer. She just looked at him. So he said, "Tell you what, I won't watch or even peek if you'll join me by the fireplace after your bath and we'll have hot chocolate and popcorn. I'll even pop it in my grandpa's ancient popcorn popper. When we were little kids, we all thought that popper was the grandest thing."

"I think *you're* the grandest thing, Tom," and Kaye couldn't think of a grander thing than sharing hot chocolate and popcorn with Tom Scott. She realized that sharing times like this with Tom was something she would always cherish more than fancy dinners in any candlelit restaurant.

Kaye was in the middle of her bath when she remembered to call her grandmother Katie.

"Who was on the phone?" Roth asked.

"It was Kaye. She's at Tom's."

"What's she doing there? She was complaining about being stuck in the same clothes for three days every time she called home. You'd think she'd come home and at least change before she went over there."

"Oh, Roth," Katie scolded, "don't be so grumpy! Why would she want to be with us frumpy old people when she has a fiancé to spend time with? Besides, she told me she stopped at Wal-Mart and bought some clean clothes. She told me Tom's got his grandparents old cook stove there and the reservoir's full of water, so she's able to get a warm bath."

Katie's explanation brought on another round of Roth's worrisome banter. "She's taking a bath at Tom's?! We can't let anyone know about this! Why, she's a schoolteacher! Doesn't she realize what people would say if they found that out?"

"Well, I guess we just won't tell anyone, Roth."

"That's for sure. I'm gonna have to explain a few things to that boy."

"No, you won't Roth! I think they understand everything they need to know." Then Katie smiled at him with a smile that conveyed the message: 'Simmer down! The world's not ending.'

Katie—she was always so calm and understanding. Roth wondered how he had ever deserved a life with a woman like her? He said, "You're right. They're two grown people. Come here gal. We've got a few hours alone here. Let me explain some things to you." Katie smiled and went and sat on his lap.

"What could you possibly tell me that I don't already know?" she asked.

"I'll think of something," he said as he untied her apron.

"What are you doing?" she asked.

"Do you need me to explain it?" Roth chuckled.

"No, not at all," and Katie kissed him with a passion that had never ceased to send sparks at lightning speed through every sensory path Roth had.

Roth wondered, with amazement, how this could still happen to a guy in his seventies. He gave a brief thought of thanks for his blessings and then wondered if they could still survive a round of sex on the kitchen table like they did years ago, or would he have trouble continuing to eat there. He decided he could doubly enjoy any meal served there and besides, the bedroom just seemed too darn far away.

Katie and Tom watched the fire and listened to the popcorn exploding in the antique popcorn popper. When there were no more popping sounds, Tom took the blackened popper out of the flames. Katie held a large bowl while Tom carefully emptied the fluffy white kernels into it, trying hard not to cover them with soot.

They decided the kitchen was a lot warmer than the living room. So they took the bowl and set it on the kitchen table each taking a chair, Tom at the end of the table and Kaye sitting to his left at the table's side, making the popcorn bowl within easy reach of each of them.

Through a mouthful of popcorn Tom said, "Now, about that wedding date."

Kaye took a sip of her hot chocolate and asked, "How soon in June would you like to have it?"

"June?! Oh, that's six months away! Can't we make it earlier than that?"

"When would you like it to be?"

"How about next week? We could slip off to Gatlinburg and get married in one of those little chapels down there."

"You can't be serious!"

"I am. Every time you leave here I get this empty feeling that I can't stand. I want you coming back here to me, to this place as your home, not going to your grandparents. I'm almost jealous of them and that's a crazy way to feel."

"Oh, Tom! While I love what you are saying, do you have any idea how disappointed my family would be if we eloped? My mother and grandmother would never forgive me, and you'd have a black mark on you from the get-go with my dad and granddad."

"Yeah, you're right. I do know that. I guess these few days of your being stranded in Lexington just have me on edge."

"Is it that Chris was stranded at the same motel that's bothering you?"

"I guess it did bother me some. NO, I don't guess. I **know** it did."

"Tom, let me tell you what I feel when I see him. I feel complete betrayal and deception. Seeing him makes my stomach queasy. I don't wish him any ill will, but I wouldn't be disappointed at all if I never had to lay eyes on him again. Tom, he's a liar, a sneak, and a cheat and thank goodness I found that out before it was too late, and I married the asshole."

"Asshole?! Whoa! I never heard you use a word like that!"

"Well, it fits!"

"If you say so."

"I do! So can we stop talking about the asshole and talk about us? Because now, in addition to having all these bad feelings, I am going to have to pray to be forgiven for calling someone a bad word. It's been a very hurtful experience, Tom, but I have to think that God was actually on my side by getting me out of that mess before I was totally devastated by it. Plus, in that prayer asking for forgiveness, I need to say a prayer of thanks for God directing me toward this small town, letting me get a wonderful teaching job and, best of all, arranging for me to come into your life."

"Gee, Kaye. You have quite a way of looking at things," and he reached out and took her hand.

"Perhaps. Now, when would you like the date for the wedding to be set?"

"Tell you what, you talk with your Mom and Grandma and set the date. I'll go along with anything you say regarding the wedding providing..."

"Providing what?"

"That you come over here and get into this old bed with me." The bed was one that had always been in a corner of the big old kitchen in Tom's farmhouse. "Maybe they will get the electricity restored out here soon. The wood cook stove has this room reasonably warm. You won't get cold in here."

"I was hoping you wouldn't let me get cold," Kaye returned.

"I won't," Tom assured her. "Wonder how many of my ancestors were conceived in this bed?"

"Oh, gee! It has a history?"

"I don't know that it has that kind of history. That's not really something my family would have discussed with me. I'm just speculating,"

"Well, we can work on adding to the number of conceptions a little later, right now I better keep up the birth control pills if I want to keep my job with any kind of respect. Besides, I braved an ice storm to go get those pills."

Then those thoughts of a couple of kids building snowmen out in the yard brought a smile to Kaye's lips.

Tom told her, "When you smile like that, you are so beautiful."

It was then that Kaye knew for sure that making love with Tom would always be her favorite thing in the world to do.

Chris made it back to his parent's house with no problems. The streets in Lexington were mostly cleared from the ice storm. He had just gone into the foyer when he heard his mother and sister engaged in what appeared to be an argument.

"Well, I like her, Mom. She seemed genuinely nice."

"I'm not debating that she was or is a nice person. She was and she is nice. She just wasn't right for Chris. He couldn't be happy and reach his full potential in some little hick town like the one where she decided to take that teaching job. He would have been a two-bit lawyer at best."

"So, I guess you think this cheerleader is a better choice?"

"Oh, I don't know, Louisa."

"Well, mother, she comes from a wealthy family and probably wouldn't have to work a day in her life if she didn't want to. Wonder if she wants to spoil that perfect figure by having kids?" Louisa interjected with an elevated sarcastic tone.

"All right, Louisa. We've said enough. Kaye and Chris are over and done with and I don't see the value in us having this argument."

"Chris is my brother, Mom, and believe it or not, I can think of someone else besides myself sometimes. All I want is for him to be married to someone who will value and love him for who he is—not for the position he can offer her in the community or for how well he can fling money at her—and I'm not sure this cheerleader can do that."

"You know, Louisa, there just might be a few cheerleaders in this world who end up in happy marriages," her mother countered.

"I'm not debating that, mother. I am not even putting all cheerleaders down. I am just very uncertain as to the motive of <u>this</u> one with my brother. **My brother**, whom I love a lot and hold very dear. If she hurts him, I will not be at all pleased with her."

Chris decided it was time to end this debate by making his presence known. When he walked in the room his mother said, "Oh, Chris, thank goodness you're home and safe."

Chris' thoughts were, *Home, yes. How safe I am in this household is questionable. I might have been safer out in that ice storm.* He was sure Kaye felt much safer wherever she was and he suspected it was at Tom's. She was definitely safe both mentally and physically at her grandparents. What a family she had. Chris couldn't help but envy her.

Chris decided he would do a little mental sword fighting with his mother. "You'll never guess what happened at the motel where I was stranded."

"What?" his mother questioned.

"I ran into Kaye. She came to Lexington to do some shopping and got stranded at the same motel."

"What a coincidence," his mother returned.

"Coincidence it might have been, mother, or maybe I was supposed to see her so I could fully realize what a fool I'd been to let her get away. And by the way, Louisa, don't worry about the cheerleader or any other gold digging female seducing or trapping me into an unhappy marriage. If losing Kaye has taught me anything, it is that I now know how careful I have to be in selecting a wife. If I ever find another Kaye Mason, Mom, I'll never let her go."

Chris did an about-face, left the room and went to his bedroom. He laid on his bed for some time and let the tears roll down the side of his face. He envied Tom Scott more than he could say.

Chapter 2

Kaye's Mom and Dad were enjoying a quiet dinner at home when Bill said, "Jean, I've been thinking. Now that Kaye has graduated from college, is out on her own, and supporting herself, that maybe we ought to start planning where we'd like to retire." Bill Mason's suggestion to his wife was met with raised eyebrows.

"Don't you think we're a little young to retire?" Jean countered.

"I don't mean quit everything, just ease back a little and pursue some other things,"

"Like what?"

"Well, I know you're very aware that Dad's health is not very good. When we were at their place during Christmas, I realized just how much I treasure the home place. Kaye will not be with them much longer. When she and Tom marry she'll go to live at his farm and I think Mom and Dad are going to need extra help with everything pretty soon."

"Are you suggesting we move there? What about our hardware business? We've worked pretty hard to make it a success."

"That's the 'ease back' part. Jim Johnson has been managing the store quite well lately and he's proposed buying the business and having us carry the mortgage. That way he'd make monthly payments to us, giving us a monthly income. Our home here is paid for. We could sell it and invest the money, or, we could even rent out this house and have more monthly income. It could be possible for us to save quite a lot if we did that. Plus, I could help Dad work the farm and that would provide more income. With the savings we already have and when we turn sixty-five and start drawing social security, I think we should make it just fine."

"Look, Bill, this is a lot to think about," Jean expressed with ample concern. Then she added, "It means moving—uprooting from all we've established here—and have you discussed this with your parents? What do they say about it? Why, I wouldn't even know what to do with all our furniture."

"I haven't discussed any of it with anyone but you. I, of course, want you to be in agreement before I take any action in that direction," Bill replied. "And I certainly haven't gotten as far as thinking about furniture and other belongings. But here's something else to think about. Kaye's marrying Tom. Hopefully, there will be grandchildren. If we lived there, we'd get to be a bigger part of their lives and I don't know about you, but I'd like that very much."

"That's true. But I believe we'll have a year or two at the very least before we have to worry about grandchildren."

"You're right, of course. Just think about it for the future. I know Bob would never want to move back there. I don't know what my brother wants anymore. He's sort of been a loner since his wife died."

"Give me some time to think about this, Bill. You're not suggesting we do this any time soon, are you?" Jean asked.

"No, not anytime soon, Jean. Take all the time you want to think it over."

"Bill, I get the feeling that this is something that you really want. Would it make you happy?" Jean really wanted to know if it would, or was Bill just doing this out of concern for his aging parents and his Dad's ailing health.

"I am concerned about Dad, and about Mama, too. How would she manage that big farm all by herself if something happens to Daddy?"

"I don't know. But, Bill, this has to be something you're doing that will make you happy, not just to ease your mind about your aging parents. Maybe your mom wouldn't want to stay on the farm once Roth dies. You know she could sell it and downsize to a more manageable place. She might just want to do that. Do you have any idea of what she might actually want to do if Roth precedes her in death?"

"No, like I said, I have had no discussions about any of this with anyone but you. You needed to be given the courtesy of being the first one I discussed it with."

"Bill, I appreciate that. I will think about all of this and talk with you later. It's a lot to wrap my mind around right now. Let's get Kaye's wedding over with before we start rearranging *our* lives. I'll have enough to do with planning that wedding for a while."

"You're right, of course. Have they set the date yet? Last I heard they had not."

Just then the phone rang and it was Kaye. "Mom, Tom and I want to set our wedding date. Let's talk."

Jean smiled at Bill and put the phone on speaker.

Bill and Jean agreed that they would drive to Roth and Katie's farm over the next long weekend that Kaye had off from school. That would be Martin Luther King Day near the end of January.

Roth and Katie were getting to see and enjoy their family a lot more lately. Bill and Jean's visits were more frequent since Kaye had moved in with them and began her teaching job.

The long weekend would give Kaye and Jean and Grandma Katie three days to begin planning Kaye and Tom's wedding. Jean and Katie went into high gear. Katie began buying bride magazines and Jean put announcements in the papers in Paducah where they lived, in the paper in Lexington where Kaye had attended college and had lots of friends, and in the local paper that served the rural area of Hope Springs.

Chris' mother, Mrs. Wilshire, opened the Lexington Herald Leader each morning checking out the society page first before moving on to local and national news. "Oh, look, Louisa. Kaye Mason's engagement has been officially announced."

"Where's Chris, Mother? Has he already left for work?" Louisa asked, standing up and looking frantically at the kitchen door.

"No, Louisa, he has not left yet. Why are you so upset?"

"Surely you're not going to show that to him before breakfast, Mother."

"Well, I don't see why not. He knows she's engaged."

"You just enjoy rubbing salt into wounds, don't you, Mother? Please hide that paper before Chris comes down to breakfast."

"For heaven's sake, Louisa. Do calm down. I can hardly stop Chris from reading the paper. I'm sure he probably has another copy at his office. Besides, I doubt seriously that he is a faithful reader of the society page."

"Mother, there's no need in destroying his breakfast. He's been noticeably depressed since the ice storm when he saw her and learned she was engaged. Leave him alone this morning. He doesn't need to hear from us that her engagement has been announced."

Chris had barely gotten into his office and hung up his coat when Arnold Samuels, another new hire at the law firm, came into his office. They had both attended law school at the University of Kentucky and had been in the same fraternity, so they had attended a lot of the same parties during their years at the university. "Hey, Chris, didn't you used to date a girl named Kaye Mason?"

"Yes. Why?"

"If I remember correctly, you two were pretty serious weren't you?"

"We were. Why are you asking?"

"Her engagement and wedding announcement is in today's paper," Arnold answered.

"Oh? I hadn't looked at the paper yet this morning. Since when did you take up reading the society page? I thought death, estate trusts, and wills were your thing."

"Oh, gee guy, you sound a little down. I really didn't come in here trying to upset you. I just recognized the name."

"It's nothing, Arnold." Chris did a cover up by saying, "The Blanchard case has me a little on edge. It's not going as well as I want and I knew about Kaye's engagement. Don't be concerned. Her engagement is not something I am giving much thought to at all right now."

"Okay, guy. Let me know if there's anything I can do to help on the Blanchard case. Be glad to do it," and Arnold backed out the door, closing it behind him.

The paper was on Chris's desk and he picked it up and threw it against the wall. He wasn't about to read about what he had lost.

Chapter 3

School was only delayed two days before resuming after the Christmas break. Kaye was glad to see that there was no evidence that the building had ever been used as a shelter during the ice storm.

As usual during a holiday from school, people use the time to move, and there were several people at a table in the front hall filling out enrollment papers for new students. Kaye wondered if Cory Wilson was being enrolled in another school this morning. She had not received notice that Cory had been withdrawn from her roll yet. It probably would not arrive for a few days. Kaye knew that he and his brother Jason had been placed with their grandparents in another school district. This occurred after his mother was hospitalized during Christmas break due to a physically abusive episode from Cory's father. It had left her with some fairly serious injuries.

Kaye collected her mail from her in-house mailbox and noticed a note from the counselor.

Kaye,
  Cory's mother and grandparents want to meet with us after school today. Please stop by my office and let me know if you can stay.
          Mrs. Adams
          Counselor

Kaye stopped by Mrs. Adams office and told her she'd be glad to stay. "Good. I'll phone and tell them."

"Do you know what this is about?" Kaye inquired.

"No, Kaye. I really don't. Guess we'll find out this afternoon."

Kaye walked on to her room and started reviewing her lesson plans for the day. Abby, the attendance clerk appeared at her door and announced, "Miss Mason, you have a new student." The clerk looked a little strange as she approached Kaye with the enrollment paperwork.

When Kaye looked beyond the clerk to the student and the mother, she understood why. The child was fairly clean and dressed reasonable well, but the mother was in an ill- fitting outfit that was way too large for her tiny frame. Plus, Kaye wasn't real sure, but the lady appeared to be wearing a pair of combat boots that even though they laced up her legs, it was apparent that they too were much too large for her and she was having a lot of difficulty walking in them.

"Miss Mason, this is Cammy Jo Brown and her mother, Sara," the clerk stood with her back to the new student and her mother and looked over her glasses so that her eyes met Kaye's, trying to clearly convey the message: 'This situation is *really* strange!'

Kaye swallowed her apprehension, stepped forward, put her hand on Cammy Jo's shoulder, and said, "I am so pleased to have you in my class, Cammy Jo. It's nice to meet you, Mrs. Brown," and she shook the mother's hand. "Cammy Jo, let's get you settled into a desk and get you the books you need."

Cammy Jo's mother stepped forward and said, "I'm sorry, Miss Mason, but I have no school supplies to bring with Cammy Jo today. I'll work on trying to get them to you within the next couple of days."

"Oh, I'm sure we can make out until then, Mrs. Brown. Please don't worry about it."

The attendance clerk said, "Well, we have several more students registering today who need to be assigned to rooms. I need to go back to the office. If you will follow me, Mrs. Brown, I'll escort you back to the front of the building. That is unless you have something more to discuss with Miss Mason."

Mrs. Brown looked at Kaye and Kaye could tell there was more Mrs. Brown needed to say, but couldn't bring herself to do so at that time. Mrs. Brown hung her head and said, "No, nothing else right now," and followed the attendance clerk out the door after giving Cammy Jo a very tightly squeezed hug.

Cammy Jo gave Kaye a heart-melting smile and settled into her desk while Kaye collected books, pencils, and paper for her to use. The buses started arriving and the students filtered in. Kaye was glad to see that all of her students had returned except Cory.

Kaye introduced Cammy Jo to the other students and assigned her a 'buddy' to help her acclimate to the new environment. The new student was proving to be a model of manners and seemed to be accepted very well among the other little girls in the class.

The school day came to an end and Kaye escorted Cammy Jo to her bus. When Cammy Jo was about half way across the parking lot, she turned around and gave Kaye a little goodbye wave and what could be described as half of a smile. Kaye smiled and waved back.

Mrs. Adams was waiting for Kaye in her office along with Cory's mother and grandparents. Mrs. Wilson looked very uncomfortable and Kaye felt just as uncomfortable. After seeing a newscast of the woman's husband being taken away in a police car to jail and an ambulance containing Mrs. Wilson pulling away from the scene, Kaye wasn't sure what to say.

She shook the grandparents' hands and said, "Hello, I'm Cory's teacher, Miss Mason. Glad to see you again, Mrs. Wilson," and she took a seat in the only vacant chair in the office.

Mrs. Adams took the lead in getting the communication started. "You requested a conference with Miss Mason and me. That usually is due to some kind of concern, so how may we help you?"

The grandparents started to talk but Mrs. Wilson raised her hand, cutting them off and said, "No, please. Cory is my child and I truly need your support, Mom and Dad, but I need to be the one to speak." There was a moment of quiet where everyone seemed to fidget while Mrs. Wilson collected her thoughts and courage.

"I'm sure you more than likely saw that horrible news broadcast of me being hauled away in an ambulance and Mr. Wilson being taken away in handcuffs to jail."

Kaye and Mrs. Adams looked at each other and then both nodded yes that they had witnessed the televised episode of this family's very private problems being made public. "Well, as you can see, I am out of the hospital. I am working with a spouse abuse counselor. Cory's father is also receiving some psychiatric help. He, however, is not allowed to be near his family again until his doctors have released him. There was an emergency hearing and the judge has issued a restraining order. Several changes have taken place in our family. The boys and I have the right to stay in our home. My Mom and Dad have generously agreed to assist me with house payments until such time that I can make it on my own. A social worker has been assigned to us and she is assisting me in getting funds to return to school and finish my degree. I had a couple of years of credit before I quit to raise my family. The social worker is also helping me to find part time employment to assist with bills until I can finish my degree. The boys' father will have to contribute to the boys' financial welfare. He has been allowed to return to work on a work release program, but must report back to a halfway house each afternoon after his job hours and on weekends. I do not plan on allowing him back into our house. I say house rather than home because it's never been the kind of home it should have been for me or for the boys."

"Now, having said all that, what our main concern in coming here is that when Cory and Jason return to school, and they want to come back to their schools, the ones they are familiar with, that there will be problems. Mainly, if the other children have seen that newsflash or heard their parents talking, my children might face some humiliating circumstances and gossip. My spouse abuse counselor has suggested that we see you and discuss what can be done to prevent this from happening."

Mrs. Adams responded with, "I see, and did the counselor have any suggestions for how to accomplish this?"

Mrs. Wilson came back with, "Yes, she did. She suggested that Cory's teacher discuss the situation with her class and set up a barrier to the comments that the kids might make to Cory regarding this."

"That's all well and good, Mrs. Wilson. I'm sure Miss Mason could do this, but you must realize that that would only insulate Cory from comments other students would make in Miss Mason's classroom. It would be impossible to protect him everywhere. I mean what about on the bus and other places where he'd be exposed to students not in Miss Mason's class?"

Mrs. Wilson answered, "We know you can't protect him everywhere, but he will spend most of his time in Miss Mason's classroom, and if he has to sit in there hours at a time with a child who has made him really uncomfortable or mad, with even a comment that may or may not have been meant to be hurtful, he will suffer emotionally and possibly academically. He'll be focused on his hurt and anger rather than on his lessons, and then we will have another problem with him failing his subjects," Mrs. Wilson explained.

"You have a point, Mrs. Wilson," Mrs. Adams agreed. "Kaye, I believe it's your turn to speak."

"I will have to think about how I'll approach the other students with this, but I'll do my best, Mrs. Wilson. And I also want to say that I have to admire the strides you have made and steps you are taking to help yourself and your sons."

"Thank you. I'd like to keep Cory home one more day; actually he's still at his grandparents for now. My sister is with the boys while we are here. I would like to get my boys back to their house and to their routine as soon as possible. So, if you will speak to your class tomorrow, I will send Cory back to school day after tomorrow. As for the bus, I know I can't protect him forever, but

I'll transport him to and from school for a couple of weeks until this mess has had some time to die down."

"I'll do my best Mrs. Wilson," Kaye assured her.

Mrs. Adams added, "Please see that we get copies of the restraining order, Mrs. Wilson. Until we have that on file here at the school, we cannot legally prevent Cory's father from seeing him, and a worse nightmare for you might be that we can't prevent him from signing him out of school, and I have to believe you really do not want him doing that."

"Oh, no! Definitely not! I will see that you get copies day after tomorrow when I bring Cory to school," Mrs. Wilson assured them.

With that, Mrs. Wilson and her parents stood to leave, shook hands with everyone, said thank you and left. Mrs. Wilson, however, returned to the door and said, "Thank you again. I know this is awkward for you," and she turned and left once more.

Mrs. Adams and Kaye just looked at each other for a moment before either could speak. Then Mrs. Adams said, "Can't possibly be as awkward for us as it is for her. You handled that well, Kaye."

Kaye's response was, "Let's hope I handle tomorrow and Cory's future days as well. But you know what, Mrs. Adams? I think I'm going to be less worried about Cory's situation now. Mrs. Wilson seems to be headed in the right direction."

"Let's hope so, Kaye."

Kaye went to the office to check her mail to find the attendance clerk still working, "You're working late, Abby."

"Yes, Kaye. Come in here a minute."

"Okay. You seemed flustered when you brought me my new student today."

"Well, yes, and that's why I want to talk to you. You saw how that mother was dressed. Do you think she's mentally stable?"

"I don't know, Abby. It was strange. You have to wonder where she got those clothes. Yet she spoke with much better oral English grammar skills than you would have expected."

"That's true, Kaye. I just have a very funny feeling about this. I know the address she gave and it's back at the very end of a road where some very 'unusual' characters live. The house is in shambles and the reputation of the guys who live there is anything but good. I can't figure out why this woman would be there, and according to the registration form, Cammy is only one of two kids belonging to this woman. There is one younger than Cammy. Kaye, this just can't be a good situation."

"Apparently not, but Cammy seems to be a real sweet kid," Kaye responded.

"Well, that's good. I just have a feeling that we will be dealing with this situation a lot more in the future."

"I guess we'll see, Abby. You don't stay too late, now. I know we had a bunch of new students to enroll today. You've got to be swamped."

"Yes, several enrolled and some have moved from our district and have to be removed from the rolls. I am a little behind with my work now, but I'll catch up. Don't tell anyone I'm here. You know I'm not supposed to put in overtime and not get paid, but I have to get these finished or tomorrow I'll be so swamped that I will never be able to catch up."

"Won't tell a soul." Kaye left the office wishing the school system had funds to reward people like Abby who were willing to work overtime hours with no pay in order to get their jobs done. She also wondered how kids ever learn anything with all the problems they bring in from outside the classroom. She thought, *Here I have one student with a dad who beat the hell out of his mom and now a new one with a mother in an outfit that looks worse than something she could have possibly found from Goodwill, and clumping around in a pair of big floppy combat boots to boot.*

It was time to go home and see what Grandma Katie had fixed for dinner. There were, after all, some parts of Kaye's life that were much more pleasant than what she'd been experiencing today.

Kaye entered her grandma's kitchen to the usual smells of home cooked delights.

"Kaye, good to see you. Would you set the table? I'm running a little behind here. I'm trying a new recipe for apple dumplings and I didn't allow enough time to get everything done when it should be."

"Oh, Grandma, I'm sure no one will starve if supper is delayed a few minutes," Kaye tried to assure her grandmother. "Might put a little spice into the routine around here. Besides, I'm sure the apple dumplings will be worth the wait."

"Well, I hope so. But you know how your grandfather is about being on time."

"Oh, goodness, Grandma, don't tell me he hasn't been late for supper at least a few times in his life."

"Not very many, Kaye. When you get the table set, call him to dinner. I'll put all the food on the table while you do your part." With that Kaye gathered plates, silverware and napkins and proceeded to the dining room. She found her grandfather already there.

"Supper's running a little late tonight. Was Katie waiting on you, Kaye?"

"No, Granddad. I've instructed her never to do that. She's made a new dessert that took more time than she anticipated, but from the smell in the kitchen, I'm sure it will be worth the delay. Here, put these plates around, and I'll do the silverware and napkins." Kaye watched with amusement, as she knew her grandfather was seldom called upon to assist with any kind of household task. In this household, men's work was men's work and women's work was women's work and the two seldom crossed paths.

Katie appeared with the food and all three were soon seated and saying grace. Kaye knew her grandfather knew most everyone in the county, so she described where her new student lived and asked if he knew the people who lived there.

Her grandfather laughed and began telling her stories about the 'characters' that lived at the end of the road the attendance clerk had described to Kaye when she was in the clerk's office after school. Abby had described them as characters and apparently she hit the nail on the head. These folks were 'something else' according to her grandfather.

Roth told about an incident where one of the guys had hit a tree in a neighbor's yard. The neighbor rushed out to the car and said, "Are you hurt?" The guy opened the door, got out of the car and said, "Hell, no. I stop like this all the time," took a few steps and passed out cold.

The ancestors of these people were known for bootlegging, but Roth said he didn't think that was happening anymore. Both men living there were brothers and had inherited the property, such that it was. Plus, they both worked at the local distillery and employees who bootlegged weren't well received.

Kaye found her grandfather's stories amusing, but decided she would most decidedly keep an eye on Cammy Jo.

Chapter 4

Tom received a notice in his mailbox to pick up a package that had arrived and was being held for him at the post office. He hadn't ordered anything and couldn't imagine who would be sending him a package. Besides, most everything he ordered was some kind of a part for a piece of farm equipment that he was repairing. Those things seldom came by regular mail. UPS or Fed Ex usually delivered them.

He had to go to town for some horse feed and a few other supplies today, so he'd make the stop at the post office while he was there. Tom took his hired hand, Frankie, with him to assist. He gave Frankie a list of places he needed to go and the things he needed to get. He told Frankie, "Maybe if both of us put our efforts together, I won't get back home and discover I forgot something."

Frankie was more than glad to help and he needed some things, too. Lately, gasoline was at such a premium, it would save him some money to ride along with Tom. As they were passing the diner in Hope Springs Tom said, "It's real near lunch time, Frankie. I skipped breakfast this morning and my belly button feels like its about to meet up with my backbone. Let's get some lunch."

The diner wasn't too crowded, as most of the businesses in town had not yet released employees for their lunch hours. The new waitress, who had replaced Marty, looked like she was too young to know what she was doing, but much to Tom's surprise, she took their order and delivered their food with unexpected efficiency. He just wished she'd get rid of the wad of gum she kept popping around in her mouth.

Jerry and Julie Mayhugh were seated at the table beside Tom and Frankie and Jerry made the comment while the waitress was back in the kitchen filling the orders that the girl was cute enough and efficient, but she sure wasn't Marty. Jerry and Julie were friends of Tom's and well known for their talent with bluegrass music. Tom tinkered a little with the banjo and they had all had an impromptu jam session at Roth and Katie Masons' house one night last spring.

Jerry and Julie had not heard about Tom and Kaye's engagement and they knew that Tom made regular stops at the restaurant when Marty had worked there as a waitress before she had gotten the scholarship to study art in Paris. He had also purchased Marty's box supper at the fund raising event held at the elementary school last year. So Jerry asked, "Have you heard from Marty lately, Tom? How's she doing over there in Paris?"

"You know, Jerry, I haven't heard from her in several months. She sent a postcard with the Eifel Tower on it and a message that she made the trip over all right and was settled in a flat somewhere near the university where she is studying," Tom replied.

Julie added, "Well, I sure would have liked to have had that painting she donated to the school auction last year, but it brought way too much money for me to be able to afford it at the time. I heard she left a bunch of paintings here that she hasn't sold. She was living with Mrs. Givens when she left here. Do you think she has those paintings? I wonder if Marty would be willing to sell any of them. You know she might need the money being so far away from home and all."

Tom knew where the paintings were. He hadn't thought about them for a while. He remembered going through them after placing them in his spare bedroom upstairs right before Marty left.

Caution lights began flashing for Tom. Should he tell Julie he had the paintings? He had not even thought about them for a while, as he seldom went upstairs. He just didn't use that room and that was why he had offered it to Marty as a storage place for her artwork. Now what was he going to do? Should he contact Marty and see what she wanted to do with the paintings? He couldn't keep them without letting Kaye know they were there. Eventually, she would discover them. He was more than sure that when he and Kaye married she would clean the house, including the upstairs bedroom and you couldn't miss seeing the paintings. There were stacks and stacks of the things.

Frankie knew about Tom's engagement to Kaye and even though he didn't know Tom had the paintings, he could tell that Tom was a little uncomfortable with the conversation that was taking place. He wasn't one to pry, however, and accepted that if Tom wanted to talk to him he had every opportunity to do so just about anytime he wanted.

Now Tom had to decide if he would tell Julie he had the paintings or wait until later to tell her. He knew that if he waited that it might seem a little odd that he didn't just tell her right off the bat today that the things were at his house. He decided that honesty was the best policy and made some mental notes to take care of this situation before it had any kind of a chance to get out of hand.

"Julie, I will see if I can locate Marty's information and give it to you so you can contact her. I actually have her paintings stored in a room upstairs at my house. Mrs. Givens couldn't keep them, as she needed to rent Marty's room out as soon as possible after Marty left. She depends on that rent money in order to make ends meet, if you know what I mean."

"Oh, I know what making ends meet means! I certainly do, Tom. Thanks. I will look forward to getting in contact with Marty when you find her contact information, and I will also hope she doesn't want an arm and a leg for her paintings. I, too, have to make ends meet."

After finishing lunch Frankie reminded Tom that they had one more stop to make that was on his list. "What's that?" Tom asked.

"The Post Office, it says here, on this list that you made." Frankie replied.

"Oh, yeah, that's right." When Tom emerged from the Post Office he holding a long cylinder.

"Well, what in the world is that, Tom?"

"Don't really know, but it is from Paris, France, so it must be from Marty. Seems like she is the topic of the day."

"I bet it is another one of those paintings Miz Julie was talking about."

"Could be, but it better be a water color, the way it is packaged. I can't imagine that she would ship an oil or acrylic painting like this. Don't know much about paintings, but oil and acrylics are usually done on a canvas that is stretched between some boards and I can't imagine they would survive too well being rolled up in this tube thing."

"Probably not, but even a water color might have to be handled with some special care. Isn't it done on special paper, too?"

"Damned if I know, Frankie. I do know that oil paintings take a lot of time to dry, sometimes several months. I guess we will have to solve the mystery when I get home and open this thing."

"Well, now you have my curiosity working overtime. You are gonna have to let me know what's in there. Hey, if it is a painting from Marty, what are you gonna do with it? What do you think Miz Kaye will say about it?"

"Haven't a clue, Frankie," Tom responded and then thought, *This day just keeps getting more and more complicated somehow and I need to decide just exactly what I am going to do with all those paintings. I am sure Kaye will not be at all interested in keeping them. I can just see our walls decorated with paintings done by another woman I have dated.*

When Tom got home, he and Frankie put supplies away and then Tom took out his knife and said, "Okay, Frankie, let's solve the mystery."

"Thought you'd never get around to it. Been dying to know what's in that tube."

Sure enough it was a watercolor of a beautiful French countryside that Marty had painted. Inside was a letter that said:

Dear Tom,

France is more than I ever dreamed it could be. Wish you were here with me. We could do so many wonderful things together.

The classes at the university are terrific. I feel like my artwork has jumped ahead by leaps and bounds. I've sent you this picture to see if you agree.

My year to study here will soon be coming to an end. I'm sad to say it has all gone way too fast. Other than missing my friends like you in Hope Springs, I keep thinking that leaving France is going to break my heart.

I have been able to take weekend jaunts by Euro rail to several other places since I have been here. The European countries are so enchanting and offer so many scenes worthy of painting. I wish I were rich and could afford to spend my life traveling and painting. But alas, the practical side of life always emerges and I need to earn money in order to live.

I am happy to get to tell you that I have sold several paintings since I came here. A gallery that works with the university displays them and that's been my avenue toward sales. My command of the French language has improved and I plan to visit some of the local art shops to see if they will be willing to offer my work for sale.

I have been approached by an agent who would be willing to handle my sales, for a percentage, of course. He is connected to an agency in the states and I may work a deal with them to take the paintings I left with you, so they could be placed for sale. The only problem is I don't know if the agency will want them. They are my earlier works, the ones I painted before this year of instruction.

You probably would like to get those paintings out of your way. I will let you know more about the agency that might sell them as soon as I can arrange some kind of a deal with them.

I'll give you a call in a few days when I know more. I have been given a deal on a cell phone through offers the university extends to foreign exchange students. I get a good break on the costs of international calls.

Well, I have chewed your ear enough about art with this letter. Be looking forward to talking to you. Know you're not much for letter writing, and neither am I. I should have kept in touch with you better this year, but I just get so absorbed in this environment. Would love to hear from you though, and thanks for keeping my paintings.

Marty

Tom was going to call Julie and tell her about Marty's letter so Julie could get in contact with Marty. Then he realized that he had Marty's address and in her letter she mentioned having a phone, but had failed to tell him what the number was.

She did say she'd call in a few days. He wondered what a few days might amount to with Marty, since it had been months since he had heard from her. He knew that mail didn't go overseas overnight. It took some time to arrive, but not months. He put off the call to Julie and decided to discuss Julie buying one of Marty's paintings with her when Marty called him.

Tom decided the next phone call he should make ought to be to Kaye. She answered, "Mason residence, Kaye speaking." Caller ID was not something in which her grandparents had invested, so Kaye was pleased to hear Tom's voice at the other end of the phone line.

"Hey, gal. How'd your first day back go?"

"Tom, the kids are great, but my college courses didn't prepare me for dealing with all these social problems."

"Oh, no. Don't tell me you're dealing with another abusive father beating the snot out of his wife again."

"Well, I had to deal with that and another situation that's hard to describe."

"Tell you what. Have dinner at my place tomorrow night and you can describe it to me then. Sounds like you need to talk about it. There's that concerned tone I'm hearing in your voice. Why don't you just come over here when you get off from work and we can fix supper together?" Tom offered.

"Sounds great! I'll be there, and Tom, it's lovely having someone who wants to hear about my problems. I hope we can always share our concerns with each other." Kaye returned gratefully.

"Oh, boy," Tom thought, "I hope my concerns don't bite me in the butt." He was making the call originally to invite Kaye to supper so he could tell her about Marty's painting. Now he'd be listening to her concerns about whatever was bothering her about her classroom. He'd just have to study Kaye's reaction and then decide from there how to proceed. He hoped he didn't overload her with concerns outside her classroom. The ones inside were probably enough for her to be dealing with right now.

Kaye got through her second day back and wondered if her talk with the class concerning Cory would have the results that Cory's mother, Mrs. Wilson, had hoped that it would. Kaye just hoped she'd handled it well. Mrs. Adams, the counselor, had told Kaye to call on her if she needed any help with explaining the situation to the students, but Kaye thought she should first try to handle it on her own. Kaye let the students have a short discussion about the situation and they decided, as a class, not to mention anything to Cory. She had faith in her students that they would stay away from the subject with Cory. Several of the students had watched the news in their homes with their parents and knew about Cory's father's abusiveness. It was a small community and news travels fast in little townships. Phone lines have a way of humming when transmitting bad news and Kaye knew this all too well.

When three-thirty rolled around, Kaye was looking forward to seeing Tom and just being with him for the evening. She had her dismissal list in her hand and was checking to see that the correct students left as each bus number was called. Cammy Jo's was the last bus number announced. Kaye decided to walk out with Cammy Jo and check her in-house mailbox while up near the school's office.

As Cammy Jo was about to exit the classroom, she turned around in the doorway, looked at Kaye and said, "Don't wurry, Myth Mathon, I'll help keep your sequit. Doze tings weally shouldn't be discussed out in pubwic."

Kaye's response was, "Oh, thank you, Cammy Jo! I appreciate that and I am sure Cory and his parents will appreciate it, too. Cory will be here tomorrow. I am sure you will like him."

Kaye was a little surprised at the grown up way in which Cammy Jo had stated this, and also made a note to see if the child was receiving speech therapy. She obviously spoke with a lisp and the speech therapist would have to diagnose all the other problems Kaye was hearing, but had no name that she could place upon them.

Cammy Jo came back with, "I am sure I will like Cory. I like ebreebody. Tings like what happen to dem are hard on a famblee."

"Yes, Cammy Jo, you're right." Kaye thought Cammy Jo's empathy was a little strong for an eight-year-old and wondered how much experience Cammy Jo had with abusive situations. The child was absolutely a joy to be around. She'd heard of falling in love with your students, but she just wanted to take this one home with her and keep her. The child just seemed bent on doing everything correctly. Kaye was trying to remember what she had read about an excessive need to please? Could this be normal or not? There was a lot yet to be learned about Cammy Jo's situation, and Kaye wasn't really sure she wanted to know everything.

She decided to discuss it with Tom. She knew he wouldn't say anything to others, and while he didn't always have solutions, he was a good listener. Sometimes a viewpoint outside the school setting proved to be valuable input. Kaye saw Cammy Jo out the door, picked up her mail and headed back to her classroom to prepare it for the next day's routine.

Tom was glad to see Kaye's little compact car come down the lane. His hired hand's wife, Miz Effie, canned food from the garden they raised together in the summer. Tom supplied the land, seeds and plants, and the machinery, plus, put in his part of the outdoor labor in exchange for Miz Effie's indoor services with the canning.

Tom was always glad to open those jars that held his own homegrown food. During the winter months those jars assured him that his diet was what he felt was better than most people enjoyed. He wasn't sure about Kaye's preferences, however, so he set out a variety of Mason jars and decided he'd let her choose what to open. He loved pickled beets, and green beans, but knew not everyone did, and he wasn't sure what Kaye liked. He'd never tried to feed her before. Usually, when they were together for a meal, it was at her grandparents, Katie and Roth Mason's. Or they were in a restaurant somewhere, and that had not occurred too often. Between his work on the farm and Kaye's responsibilities with her teaching job, neither one had a lot of time for doing a lot of dating, plus, his funds were a little limited until his crops started paying off.

He really didn't want to get into his inheritance from his father for just any old reason, but lately he thought he just might use the money for a honeymoon trip with Kaye. Now that she and her mother and grandmother would finally get together and set a date for the wedding, maybe he could find a special place to take her. He would have to do a little investigative work to find out where she might like to go. He realized he had a lot to learn about Kaye. First, if she even liked to travel, then where she might want to go, and tonight he'd learn what she liked to eat.

Kaye was amused at Tom's concern for her food preferences. She laughed and assured him that she was no picky eater. Grandma Katie had taught her to like a variety of food. She was a little amazed at the beef roast that Tom lifted from the crockpot.

"I put it in this morning," he explained.

"I see. What is all the stuff I see on it?" Kaye inquired with a slight frown.

"Herbs! I raise them with Miz Effie. I learned to put them between paper towels, place them in a microwave and dry them. So your roast has rosemary, thyme, and sweet basil on it for seasonings."

"You're kidding. You're a gourmet cook, Tom! Can I expect dinners like this after we're married?"

"I'll see what I can do."

"How'd you learn about herbs? What got you into that?"

"I've always liked to cook. Don't do it often, cooking for myself isn't much fun. But since I got this book on herbs and started growing them, I've kind of considered going organic with this farm and seeing what I could do with commercial production of vegetables and herbs."

"Wow, Tom! You're amazing! Just when I think I know you, you spring something new and unexpected at me. Most of these guys around here are tobacco and soybean croppers," Kaye said with an admiringly big smile.

"*Oh, yeah,*" Tom thought, "*Wait til I spring the Marty paintings on you. That will be 'unexpected' I'm sure. I wonder if I'll still see those big admiring eyes then?*"

Kaye selected the green beans and the pickled beets to go along with the roast. Tom had carrots in the crockpot with the roast so the meal was complete. She suggested just loading their plates from the stove rather than messing up serving bowls just for the two of them. Tom considered that quite practical and after setting down with his plate, said, "Now, tell me about what's bothering you at school."

Kaye explained about the meeting with Cory's mother and grandparents and her talk with her students. Tom looked up over his plate catching Kaye's eyes and said, "Well, I guess you'll just have to see how it goes when Cory comes back to school tomorrow."

"But Tom, let me tell you about my new student." After Kaye explained, Tom asked, "Where did you say she's living?"

"I forgot the exact address, but Granddad told me a story about the guys who live there," and Kaye related the story to Tom about the guy hitting a tree in the neighbor's yard.

"Oh, I know who you're talking about. Yeah, those guys are characters for sure. Did you say the mother was wearing combat boots?"

"Yes, at least I think that was what they were. What I do know is that they were about four sizes too big for her. At least it seemed that way."

"Well, honey, if I am thinking about the right old boys that you said she is living with, I guess she might need to put those boots right up their asses every once in a while. You have your hands full just keeping an eye on the little girl."

Kaye and Tom finished their meal in silence. Kaye seemed to be all talked out and Tom couldn't think of anything else to say. Besides, he was full of thoughts about how to tell Kaye about Marty's paintings. He wasn't at all sure that she needed to deal with paintings in his upstairs room done by another woman in his life with all the problems she was facing at her teaching job at school.

They cleared the table and did the dishes together. Kaye sensed something was bothering Tom, but thought she wouldn't pry. If he needed her advice or wanted to talk to her, he would.

"Thanks for listening to all that, Tom. I don't mean to burden your day with all my work-related problems."

"You didn't, Kaye. I want you to always share your problems with me. But there is something I need to discuss with you."

"Okay, good. I'm listening."

"Well, I don't know if it's gonna be good or not." Kaye just looked at Tom and gave no verbal return so he decided to plow ahead and hoped he didn't get buried in the furrow he was about to create. "You remember Marty, don't you?"

"Yes, the waitress at the diner. Didn't you buy her pie supper at the school auction last year, and she visited Grandpa with you when he had his surgery?"

"Yes, we dated for a while until she got the chance to go to France and study."

"She is an artist, isn't she?"

"Yes, and when she left she had several paintings at Miz Givens's house where she rented the upstairs. Miz Givens had no place to store the paintings so I offered to keep them here."

"You did? Where are they? I've never seen them."

"They're in an upstairs bedroom."

"You know I've never been in your upstairs. Let's go see the paintings," Kaye suggested, pushing her chair back from the table where they'd been sitting since finishing the dishes.

Gee, this was going better than Tom expected! Kaye didn't seem at all upset. Tom led the way to the bedroom that housed the paintings and held the door for Kaye to pass through. There were two stacks of canvases leaning against the wall. Kaye walked over to the stacks and started flipping through them. Most were landscapes and still-lifes, but then she turned to a painting of a male nude. "Oh, wow! This certainly isn't you, Tom."

"Hell, no! Absolutely not! I don't think I could be persuaded to pose for a nude painting of myself. Besides, I don't think I look quite as good as that fellow."

"Oh, I don't know about that. What are you going to do with all these paintings, Tom? Is Marty coming back and does she know about us?"

"I don't know what Marty is going to do. Seems like no one ever really does know what Marty is up to next. She sent me a postcard when she got to France to let me know she had arrived. That was the last time I had heard from her until today, and she left last spring. What is that now, seven months ago? So, no, she doesn't know about us, at least not to my knowledge. I wanted you to know about some things. So let me tell you what I do know. Her study time in France will soon end. I hadn't heard anything from her until today, other than that postcard she sent letting me know she arrived safely when she first went over there. Then today I received a package from her with a letter in it."

"A package? What did she send you?"

"Another picture. Like I need another one of those." Kaye suddenly burst out laughing and Tom looked at her rather puzzled and then started laughing, too. This was not at all like he thought Kaye might react. Then he added, "Well, she did ask me to look at the new picture and see if her year of study had improved her painting skills."

Kaye laughed again and through the laughter asked, "Well, did it?" She could see that Tom was really uncomfortable with having to show her the paintings.

"Hell, Kaye, how would I know? I'm no art critic. The picture's downstairs. You can look at it and see what you think."

"Okay, but that still doesn't help you solve the problem of what to do with all these paintings. I sure don't want to hang all of them in this house, and you can't just store them forever. I tell you what, build me my own bathroom and I'll hang the nude male picture in there." Kaye erupted with laughter again.

"Oh, no! No nude guys in your bathroom other than me, lady! Besides, I don't intend to store the paintings forever. Marty has been selling her stuff at a gallery or a shop or someplace like that in France. She said it was an art shop in her letter, whatever that means. But she has been approached by an agent who wants to market for her."

"That's good!"

"Yeah, real good for me. Marty said the agent is connected to an agency here in the states and they might want her early stuff."

"She's lucky, or maybe we should give credit to her talent. Not many working artist get a chance like that."

"You're right. Anyway, Kaye, she's supposed to call me and tell me what is going to happen. I wanted you to know about all this. You were honest with me about Chris being at the motel in Lexington. You didn't have to tell me. You could have kept it a secret and I would never have known. I appreciate you not hiding that from me and I didn't want to hide any of this from you."

"I hope we never have anything we have to hide from each other, Tom."

"Man, Kaye, I thought you might be mad or jealous or something."

"We both had relationships before we met each other. I do not want you wondering about Chris or anyone else. I just want to know that we are all right, and from what you just did, I think we are more than all right."

"Hell, girl, we're perfect! Come here!" Tom pulled Kaye into his arms and gave her a very long, tight hug and exhaled a long sigh of relief. Then said, "Let's go downstairs. I want you to read Marty's letter and even look at the picture she sent. I actually can see some difference in how she's painting now, but I don't know if her work is better or not."

As they descended the stairs, Kaye said, "I had to take some art appreciation classes for my teaching degree, Tom, but I have to admit that I don't understand or agree with a lot of the opinions. Take van Gogh, for instance, his early work like The Potato Eaters—I think it is better and more realistic than Starry, Starry Night even if his early work is rather dark and some would say depressing. The later work is full of light but to me looks like a crazy person did it. He did cut off his own ear, you know."

"Yes, I know. Suppose you do have to be on the crazy side to cut off your ear and sit out in a field with candles in your hat brim in order to see well enough to paint Starry, Starry Night."

"Oh, my, you do know about art after all, don't you?"

"Yeah, right," Tom responded and handed Kaye Marty's letter. She read the first paragraph out loud. "'France is more than I ever dreamed it could be.' Sounds like she wants to stay."

"Sure does."

"'Wish you were here with me. We could do so many wonderful things together.' Hmmm, wonder what she had in mind?"

"Holy Smoly, Kaye, could you just see me sitting at some sidewalk café, drinking some kind of strange coffee, in the heart of the Paris art district? I'd really have lots to talk about. By the way, I know what <u>Starry, Starry Night</u> looks like. What in the hell is <u>The Potato Eaters</u>?"

"Never mind now, Tom. I'll bring my college art textbook over sometime and show you. Right now let's forget Marty and Chris and go shut the rest of the world out, too, in that big old bed in your kitchen. Are you going to keep that thing in there? Seems like an odd place for a bed."

"As long as it's being put to the good use that it has been lately, it stays. You wouldn't be trying to redecorate my house already would you?"

"Expect it. Somethings gotta go."

"Oh, no. Here it comes. Don't mind too much what goes as long as *you* stay."

Tom turned back the covers on the old bed with every intention of giving her more than enough reasons to stay.

Chapter 5

Roth stood at the fence to the corral watching the young filly as Mark Elliott used the lead rope to guide the horse around the outside of the enclosure. His only thought was, *Perfection!* He couldn't remember seeing any young foal that presented a more pleasing picture than this one.

Roth was so glad that Mark was doing well enough with his stable that he needed more space for horses. Katie was even more pleased when Mark had rented their barn stalls and was using their outdoor arena to train some of his higher spirited horses. Plus, he was available to train their foal, Homespun Honey.

It was late January and Mark and the filly were blowing clouds of steam from their mouths and noses. The filly had been imprinted early on, actually from the very day she was born.

Roth looked back on that day last spring with a lot of pride when he and Katie had gone to the barn after dark and presided over the delivery of the new foal. Roth thought, *The two of us have delivered a lot of animals while living on this old farm.* And due to their age his thoughts continued with, *This filly might be the last one, but galldurnit, if I don't believe it's the best one!*

Katie had stepped right in, rubbing the new foal and helping her to stand. Honey was nursing in no time and out kicking up her heels in this very corral with her mother in just a few days.

They had all marveled at this foal. *Of course when you raise one of your own, you always think it's the grandest,* Roth thought. But this time he wasn't real certain that he was too far from wrong. Mark trained a lot of horses and even he thought they had a prize. They had named her Homespun Honey and adopted Honey as her barn name.

Honey was eight months old and so much had happened since she was born. When Roth reflected back, he began a list. *My surgery, Kaye got her job and came to live with us.* He counted it as a blessing and delight to have his own granddaughter under his roof. *Then to top that off Kaye became engaged to Tom Scott, a good boy working hard to make something.*

There was an additional blessing in Roth's life. At his age he just couldn't keep up the responsibilities and meet the workload that his farm required of him anymore. Tom had come along at just the right time with his sharecropping offer. Then Mark had rented Roth's stable and here he was getting to watch Mark train his beautiful little Honey. Actually, if she kept growing like she had, she would not end up very little at all. This horse was going to be over sixteen hands and real near seventeen if she kept it up. That is really big for a mare.

Mark interrupted Roth's thoughts with, "Think she's had enough for today and me, too, Roth. Don't want to get her too hot in this cold weather. I'm going to put her away."

"That's fine, Mark. You be sure and let me know when you are going to work her again. I love watching her. Make sure you rub her down good. She really doesn't look that hot, but don't take any chances."

"Sure thing, Roth. She's coming along nicely." Mark never liked to make promises, or say things to give people false hopes, but he thought he might have a horse on his hands that would someday be a real contender at Louisville. He didn't have much in his stable right now that he thought could do much of anything at the World Championships held each year at the Kentucky State Fair. He was looking forward to the spring sales at Tattersalls and St. Louis to see if there were any possible prospects. *You never know,* he thought, *when you might run into another Be Happy.* That horse had been purchased at Tattersalls and went in the ring at Louisville afterward and won the Fine Harness World Championship. Mark remembered that night well. Be Happy absolutely held class for the other horses in the ring and showed what being happy was all about. She enjoyed showing and set the crowd on fire with applause.

Mark had some feelers out to other stables, too, hoping something would become available. He had some riders ready to move up to more advanced classes and horses. *Who knows,* Mark thought, *I might have my best future contender at Louisville right here on the end of this lead rope. We'll have to figure out how to put on a show like Face Card did. Oh, well, a guy can dream a little, I guess.*

Roth returned to the house to find Katie in a frenzy getting ready for their weekend company. Jean and Bill would be coming to begin plans for the wedding in June. The dining room table was an array of bridal magazines and samples of invitations. *What a mess!* Roth thought as he looked at Katie with one eyebrow raised.

"Oh, don't worry. You'll get your supper, Roth. It isn't every weekend we get to have our family here and plan our granddaughter's wedding. We're just going to eat in the kitchen tonight," Katie reassured him.

"Don't mind at all. Wouldn't think of asking you to clear out this mess. It would take way too long."

"It's far from a mess, Roth Mason. It's all very well organized, so we can get these wedding preparations underway. I'd explain it all to you, but I doubt you'd find it very fascinating."

"Nope! What I'd find fascinating is how did you manage to find all this stuff in a little less than a month? And even more fascinating, how did you manage to get supper fixed in the middle of this mess?"

"First, the mess, as you call it, is in the dining room--not in the kitchen. Second, I plan well. Your supper is beef stew that I put in the crockpot this morning."

"Got to rename you, woman. Never Fail Katie. Always gets it done." With that Roth walked into the kitchen and ladled out two big bowls of stew—one for him and one for Katie. He set them on the table saying, "At your service, madam. My name is Roth, and I'll be your server this evening."

Katie just looked at him with the amusement in her eyes that he had so justly earned.

The Martin Luther King holiday from school brought an extra day over the weekend, providing just the right opportunity for Kaye, her mother, and her grandmother to begin wedding plans. Tom walked into the dining room to find three busy-as-bees ladies pouring over a wagonload of magazines and samples of everything from invitations and thank-you notes, to ways to wrap birdseed for the send off.

"Come here, Tom," Kaye coaxed. "What do you think of these invitations?"

"Looks fine to me."

"You haven't really looked, Tom. I want you to have input into all of this, too."

"Honey, whatever you select will be fine and dandy with me."

"But there's so much to decide. I mean, what about the main color for the wedding, your tux, the menu, where to have the ceremony and reception, who do you want for the minister?"

"Now you have my head hurting, Kaye. I'll agree to anything you three ladies decide, but I would like to see pictures of the tux. I have never worn one and never had a desire to look like a penguin."

"Don't be silly. We'll go pick out the tux together later."

"That's a deal, Kaye. Right now I need to see your grandfather."

Roth called from the living room, "Come on in here, Tom. Let's see if I can rescue you from all the madness going on out there."

Tom had his cap in his hand so he passed it in a semicircle in front of him, giving a little bow from the waist and escaped into the living room.

"Well, he certainly wasn't much help," Kaye mused with her lower lip stuck out in a little pout.

"Get used to it, Honey," her mother warned. "It won't get any better. He's a man."

Tom handed Roth a check, saying, "Here's payment for part of the tobacco. It hasn't all sold yet,"

Roth took it and put it in his shirt pocket without looking at it and said, "Thank you. Much obliged."

"Aren't you even going to look at it?"

"Nope. Whatever it is, it's more than I could have done after all those knives got through with me last summer. Just glad you're here to do it. Can't seem to get my feet back under me like I want yet."

"Well, I'm sure it's gonna take some time, Roth."

The phone rang and Roth volunteered to answer so the ladies wouldn't have to stop doing their wedding planning. It was Mark calling from his cell phone. He was calling to let Roth know he was going to work Homespun Honey.

Roth herded Tom through the dining room and out the door to the corral. Tom watched the action in the legs of the young filly and said, "Roth, are you thinking about a halter class at Louisville next year?"

Roth looked stunned for a moment and then replied, "Now that would be a perfect debut. Wouldn't it?"

"You ought to give it some thought."

"No need to. Hey, Mark, let Tom work her for a few minutes and you come and watch." Mark wasn't real sure he wanted to hand Honey over to Tom even though he knew Tom could handle her. He was beginning to think of the filly as his own since, up to now, only he had handled her on a lead rope.

"You need to see her from afar, Mark," Roth urged, "so we can discuss her future." Mark walked to the fence and gave Tom the lead rope. Honey didn't hesitate. She walked right off with Tom even though she didn't know him.

"Tom said we ought to aim for halter classes at Louisville next year. Watch her and see if you agree." Roth's suggestion was no surprise to Mark. He was actually enjoying watching Honey proceed around the ring with Tom and he had already been thinking about future classes with Honey.

"Suits me," Mark replied. "Do you think she can be gaited or will she stay three-gaited, Roth?"

"Not ready to make that judgment yet. Need a little more time before we start pushing in either direction. You're up to the training though, aren't you?"\

"Oh, hell, yes! A win at Louisville never hurt anybody's stable," *And this one looked like a sure bet so far* was Mark's additional thought.

"Well, let's not count our ribbons before they are attached to the bridle, but I have to admit I'm pretty excited about this little filly."

Bill Mason pulled into the driveway and Roth motioned to his son to join the three men at the corral. Bill agreed that Honey looked like she was showing a lot of promise. He also told Roth that he had pizza in the car and to invite Tom and Mark in, that there was plenty for everyone.

The kitchen in the old farmhouse was alive with discussions of a wedding and future horse shows. Mark told the others he was ordering the Tattersall's catalog and would be going to the sale later in the spring. He stated that he had several customers ready to move up from academy to good first show horses and he was hoping the sale would provide some good prospects.

"That's great, Mark! The show season should be really exciting this year. You had a big cheering section last year. Your clients really support each other quite well," Katie encouraged him, handing him a slice of pizza.

"Yes. We do have a good barn family. It's an encouraging bunch to work for. Have you thought about what you want to do as far as showing this summer, Kaye?"

"No, Mark. This wedding and my job are kind of consuming me right now. I did have a lot of fun showing last summer. I'd love to see the horses sell at Tattersalls, but I'm not financially in a position to buy and pay for the training of a horse right now."

"What if I pair you up with a family that has a real promising young rider? She's a little girl who works at my stable for part of the payment on her lessons. Her parents aren't real wealthy and I know that even if I can find her a suitable horse that's worthy of her natural ability to ride, that it will tax her parents financially. If, however, I could be lucky enough to find the right horse and could pair them with another rider, they could share the costs and both could show successfully. You would be perfect, Kaye, because this girl could show in the youth classes while you'd be showing in the adult classes. You both ride well and with the right horse we wouldn't have to bring the horse down for either one of you. If we can find a good stepped-up one, it could stay that way and all of you, the little girl, the horse and you, Kaye, could show your stuff," Mark stated with a big alluring grin to Kaye.

"Sounds like a workable plan to me," Roth added. "What do you think, Tom?" Roth was interested in seeing Tom's body language as well as hearing his reply. Mark had taken Kaye to dinner and on a couple of other dates before she and Tom decided to see only each other.

"I think that's Kaye's decision, Roth. She knows how much time it takes to ride and show successfully. Do you think you have time to ride that much this summer with the wedding and all? You gals seem fairly busy with everything right now. Will that continue to be the case or are you pretty much getting it under control?" Tom asked Kaye.

"Are you kidding? Nothing is under control at this moment," Kaye's mother chimed in, looking at Kaye with a 'don't take on too much' stare.

"I don't know, Tom. I guess it will depend on a lot of things, like how much and how quickly we can get everything done for our wedding. Plus, we don't even know if Mark has a chance at locating a suitable horse. I'll have to give this some more thought. Right now it's all too much to consider," Kaye admitted.

Mark added, "Well, the kid is Louisville material. If I can find the right horse, she could be a contender in the World Championship shows. Keep it in mind, because I am going to give my best to finding that kid a horse. If I see anything attractive in the Tattersalls catalog, I'll let you know. Maybe you and Tom can take the time to go with me to the sale."

"That sale takes place for several days doesn't it, Mark? Aren't some of the days weekdays? I could work my chores around the dates, but Kaye would have to take off from work," Tom replied.

"Oh, gee, guys we're discussing possibilities. None of this may even happen." Kaye observed. "Let's talk about something that is going to happen," Kaye said finishing her slice of pizza. "Tom, come in the dining room. I want you to see what I selected for invitations and look at some pictures of tuxedoes."

Tom smiled at the guys and dutifully followed Kaye into the dining room stating, "I'd be better at picking out a horse, I think."

Chapter 6

A couple of days passed and Tom came in from servicing his farming equipment when his stomach started commanding lunch. He didn't usually get that hungry at midday. He filled up on a bologna and cheese sandwich and wondered if Kaye would still think of him as a gourmet cook if she could see him eating that big ole hunk of bologna. The phone rang. He answered, but didn't recognize the voice.

"Is this Tom Scott?"

"Yes. Who's calling, please?"

"My name is Richard Mallory. I have been in contact with a Miss Marty Walthrup. She told me you have some of her paintings stored, and that I could come pick them up and place them in some shops to sell them for her."

"She did mention that, Mr. Mallory, in a letter she sent to me recently. She was supposed to call me and let me know more about this. I haven't heard from her since the letter."

"Well, I could come down there in a couple of weeks and take those paintings off your hands. Give me your address, Mr. Scott, and I'll locate your place with my GPS."

Tom complied, finished his sandwich and went back to the repairing and maintenance chores needed on his John Deere hay baler. He was surprised when Kaye paid him an unexpected visit after school that day. He told her about the call from Mr. Mallory.

"Tom, I don't want to seem skeptical, but has Marty called you? What if this guy takes her paintings and she get shafted and gets no money?" Kaye cautioned.

"I hadn't considered that, but no, Marty hasn't called. Maybe she will soon. Who knows about Marty. You never know when she will show up. She's not very good about staying in contact. She didn't tell me the name of the guy who was to come and get her paintings, only that he was an art agent. So maybe you are right to tell me to be cautious."

"I certainly hope she does call before this person shows up. She wouldn't be the first person to be cheated in a situation like this," Kaye added with concern.

"I feel certain that she will call soon. This guy would almost have had to be in contact with her, however, I mean how else would he have gotten my number and know I had the paintings?"

"That's true. Just be careful."

"I will. Why'd you stop by? Is something up? I'm a little surprised to see you."

"Nothing is up, Tom. I just wanted to see you."

Tom smiled and walked around the baler, wiping his hands on a shop towel. "Well, here I am. What are you seeing?"

"The guy I'm going to marry. Get cleaned up and let's go do something. I need a break."

"Are things that hard at work? What's happened?"

"Nothing out of the ordinary has happened. I just needed to be with you for a while. I love my students, but sometimes you just need to be able to talk to someone over the age of eight."

"Okay, I'm qualified and I'm available. How about we go get something to eat and then see what's happening at the Silver Saddle. We could practice some of our line dancing lessons."

"Sounds great." Kaye walked to the house with Tom and waited in the living room while he showered. Tom's house phone rang and he yelled from the shower for Kaye to answer.

"Hello. Tom Scott's residence." There was a slight silence before a female voice returned with, "Hello. Is Tom available?"

"If you can wait just a minute, I believe he will be. May I tell him who's calling?"

"Yes. This is Marty Walthrup. We are old friends."

"Oh, yes, Marty. He's been expecting your call. Don't hang up. I'll rush him. He's in the shower and should be almost finished by now."

"I could call back later if this is inconvenient," Marty offered, thinking inconvenient might be a mild word considering Tom was in the shower with a woman in the house. She was suddenly remembering the good times she and Tom had once had together before she accepted the grant to study abroad.

"Oh, no. Don't hang up. You're calling all the way from France. I know Tom needs to talk to you about your paintings."

Well, whoever she is, she knows a lot more about me than I do about her, Marty thought. The voice on the other end of the line broke into her thoughts with. "Now, don't hang up, Marty. I'm going to put the phone down and go to the bathroom to tell Tom you're on the phone. I'm sure he'll be right here."

Marty responded with, "Okay, I'll wait."

Kaye knocked on the bathroom door and Tom asked, "Who was on the phone?"

"It's Marty, Tom, and she is still on the phone. I asked her to wait for you." Tom opened the door looking Kaye in the eye to see if he could determine her reaction to the call. He saw little of nothing and walked to the living room in his bare feet and a pair of jeans. He was attempting to towel dry his hair as he walked to the living room and draped the towel around his neck just before picking up the phone to talk to Marty.

"Hey, Marty! Good to hear from you."

"Hope I'm not interrupting anything too personal, Tom."

"No, you're not. Kaye and I were getting ready to go into town for a little midweek break. We both need some 'away time' from our jobs tonight. But I'm really glad you called. A guy name Mallory, called here about your paintings."

"Yes, Richard. Did he make arrangements to come and pick them up?"

"He's going to call in a few days to do that. He said he had to make a trip south of here and could swing by on his way. Is he definitely going to take them or will he just look at them and take what he wants? There are quite a few of them, Marty."

"Yes, I know. As I understand it, he travels in a van because he transports a lot of paintings and other pieces of art that are rather large. I will see if he will agree to take all of them."

"Okay, but before he does, would you mind if Julie Mayhugh came over and selected a painting to buy? She wanted the one you donated to the school fund raiser last spring, but it brought so much in the auction that she couldn't afford it then."

"That's fine, Tom. Let her select something."

"What should I charge her? I wouldn't have a clue what to ask."

"Well, Tom, without seeing the painting she selects, neither would I. Tell you what, the painting at the spring fundraiser at the school brought a little over one hundred fifty dollars. I'll only charge her fifty dollars. Whatever she selects should be worth that."

"Okay, Marty. Will do. How should I get the money to you?"

"Did you get my painting?"

"Yes, I did. It is nice, by the way. Kaye liked it, too," Tom said looking at Kaye with raised eyebrows.

"My address is on the tube I used to mail it. Do you still have the tube?"

"Yes, I have it. I'll mail you the money as soon as I can get Julie here and have her pay for the painting."

"No hurry, Tom. I'm doing pretty well with funds over here. Between my work at the university and the paintings I've sold, I even have a small savings account started."

"That's great, Marty. When will you be coming back to the states?"

"My program of study ends in June and I really don't know what the future holds for me just yet. I should let you go, Tom. I believe you said you were getting ready to go somewhere."

"Yes, Kaye and I are going to get something to eat and then go practice line dancing."

"Kaye. Why does that name sound familiar?"

"She's Roth Mason's granddaughter. You met her last spring."

"Oh, yes. Is she still in Hope Springs? I thought she had to go back to Lexington to the university and finish her degree. Wasn't she engaged to the law student who purchased her box supper at the fund raiser?"

"She did go back to Lexington to finish her degree, but she and the lawyer broke up. She got a job here teaching in the elementary school. She took Miss Flannery's place when she retired." Kaye sensed that Tom might need some 'alone time' to talk to Marty. So she gave him a little wave and started to move toward the kitchen. Tom shook his head no, caught Kaye's hand and pulled her close to him cuddling her with his free arm around her waist.

"Kaye is going to become my wife, Marty, some time in June. If you're back by then maybe you'll honor us by coming to the wedding."

All Marty could see right then was her sitting in a church pew listening to the wedding vows of a beautiful, kind man that she had slept with. She decided to pass.

"Oh, I don't really think Kaye would want me there, Tom. Plus, I probably won't be back in time anyway. But if you'll take care of those paintings for me with Richard, I'd really be grateful. Kaye probably wants them out of the house anyway."

"I'll do it, Marty. You take care and let us hear from you here in Hope Springs every once in a while."

"I will, Tom, and thanks. Be sure to tell Kaye congratulations for me. She's a lucky girl."

"Well, I don't know how lucky she is, but I'll tell her."

"Thanks, Tom. Goodbye."

"Goodbye, Marty. You be careful over there. You hear?"

"I will, Tom," and with that Marty hung up the phone. She had been wondering what her next move should be and that phone call had certainly helped her to make up her mind. Tom Scott was no longer available. She had not met many men she would even get near the thought of marrying, but Tom was number one on her list. She realized that by not staying in touch with him this past year that she had let him slip through her fingers. After all, how long could you expect a guy to keep hanging on when you've made such little effort to stay in contact with him? But she'd only had her phone for a little while and every time she thought about calling Tom, she'd realize the time difference between France and the U. S, and know it wasn't a good time. She was at least six hours ahead of their time. Right now, however, was a good calling time, and a good decision-making time. She decided to pick up the phone and call Richard Mallory.

Richard agreed to take all the paintings--not just what he liked. In view of the circumstances Marty described about Kaye and Tom's engagement, it was a small thing to do. Besides, he knew how to discard paintings that would never sell. Somehow, though, he suspected that the favor he was extending to Marty was in his best interest. From what he had seen of Marty's work, he thought he'd have a good chance at making both himself and her some money.

He'd call Tom tomorrow and make arrangements to pick the paintings up two days from now on his way to Memphis, Tennessee. He needed to head on down to Memphis to see a new folk artist that had been referred to him. Folk art was big in New York these days and he would soon be able to buy that house he had his eye on if his contacts kept bringing him talented people. Talented people were all over the place. It was just a matter of finding them and then finding a way to manage deals with them. Artistic people usually didn't excel on the business end of getting their art to good paying markets. Richard knew this only too well. Acknowledging that, he was doing well selling their work, but he sometimes grew weary of dealing with what he called 'their artistic personalities'.

Marty, however, was different. She was, no doubt, laid back, but realistic and a bit industrious. She had done a lot in less than a year with the opportunities that were opened up to her by the grant she'd received. He thought of that house again and could envision finger-painted walls from little Martys running around all over the place. Then he loosened his tie, and quickly dismissed the idea. It was six thirty and he needed to put work away and relax for a while.

Tom looked at Kaye on their way into town to eat, reached over and took her left hand causing Kaye to turn and look directly into his eyes. "Don't you think you ought to keep both hands on the wheel?"

"I can think of a lot of places where I'd rather have my hands right now."

"You're impossible."

"You're incredible, Kaye. I was expecting you to be mad about Marty's paintings since I hadn't told you about them. Forgot about the damn things actually. I hardly ever go upstairs and when I do, I seldom go in that bedroom. Then instead of you being mad, here you are cautioning me about this guy coming to get her paintings, and worried about protecting Marty's rights."

"Well, I wouldn't want to see Marty taken by a crooked art agent, but I don't want you to keep all those paintings, Tom. Well….maybe we could keep the one of the nude guy. I think I'd still like to have that one for my bathroom."

"I thought we'd already got it straight that that picture definitely goes. You hang that thing up and the first thing I am going to do is invite your grandmother over to show her how nicely you have decorated your bathroom."

"Just kidding, Tom."

"I know. Actually, Kaye, I kind of questioned Marty about that painting when I first saw it, and she was pretty evasive. I think the guy might have been someone pretty significant from her past. She wasn't willing to tell me anything about him."

"Oh, maybe it was a bad breakup."

"I don't know."

"So the mystery goes on. Wonder if we'll ever learn the secret of the nude. Kind of like, who is the lady with the Mona Lisa smile? I wouldn't object if you hung Mona Lisa somewhere in our house."

"Yeah, right, give me a break! Mona Lisa has her clothes on! I don't intend to even try to solve the mystery of who the guy is as long as he isn't hanging around in your bathroom. I'm the only guy allowed in there."

"Are you going to come in nude?"

"Do you want me to?"

"Might be interesting."

"If I weren't so hungry, we'd skip the dinner and go back home."

"Hey, Tom. I bet we could have as much fun having sex and work off as many calories as we could line dancing."

"Stop it, Kaye. What would your students say if they heard you talking this way?"

"Are you going to tell them?"

"Hell, no!" Tom conceded as he stopped the truck in front of the Mexican restaurant that had just opened in Hope Springs and said, "Since you're being such a hot tamale tonight, I thought we'd try out this place."

"Good choice, amigo. I'm hungry, too."

"All right! Too much Spanish lingo. Get out of the truck, lady."

When they walked in Julie Mayhugh immediately waved and yelled, "Hey, Tom and Kaye, come over here and join us."

Tom looked around the restaurant and spotted the couple. He guided Kaye toward the table and upon arriving, pulled out a chair for Kaye and said, "Great, Julie. I'm glad we ran into each other. Marty called and said for you to come pick out a picture. You need to do it in the next two days because an art agent is coming to take the paintings to a shop. Marty said to charge you fifty dollars. Is that all right?"

"Sure is, Tom," Julie returned sounding delighted. "When should I come over?"

"How about around five tomorrow afternoon? I should be coming in for supper about then and you can go upstairs and pick out what you want."

"I'll be there. Think I'll bring Jerry with me. Just for a second opinion."

"You're both as welcome as can be. Come ahead."

"How are you doing, Kaye?" Jerry asked.

"Just fine, Jerry. When are we going to be treated to another jam session at Grandpas? I know he'd love it. He's doing a lot more lately. I think he's finally getting back close to something like normal after his bypass surgery."

"That's great we'll see what we can do about the jam session. Tom, you'll help us out with some banjo music, won't you?" Jerry asked.

"After the last time, I'm surprised you'd even invite me to play with the two of you again," Tom replied.

"Oh, come on, Tom. You play too well to be putting yourself down like that. We all had fun," Julie added.

"Well, I'll have more fun after I get something in my stomach. How's the food here?" Tom inquired looking at the steaming plates of Mexican delights the waitress had delivered. "It looks great!"

"It is. This is the second time we've eaten here. We came back so you know it has to be good. Sit down and order," Jerry instructed.

"Whoa, Kaye! Is that an engagement ring?" Jerry asked taking Kaye's hand and turning it right and left so he could properly admire the stone.

"Sure is, Jerry."

"You two?" Jerry asked looking from one to the other.

"Yes! Nobody else!" Tom confirmed.

"Congratulations, old buddy! When did all this happen?"

"Christmas," Kaye returned with a big smile.

"Can't believe we haven't heard, but we don't get out that often. Stay busy with the kids," Julie laughed. "They keep us on the run and out of trouble. Don't have time for much gossip. Would love to see Katie and Roth again. We have to make time for that jam session."

"Great," Kaye returned, "and bring the kids! Grandma and Grandpa would love it!"

The couples finished their meals, said their goodbyes and Kaye and Tom slugged off to the Silver Saddle to practice their line dancing feeling much too full. Tom felt full of everything. How could life have become so good for him? He had the pictures from Marty all taken care of without Kaye getting jealous, angry or hurt. He was really sweating that. Julie was getting her picture. His income was improving and his engagement was great. The daggone engagement was just lasting way too long! He wanted Kaye with him all the time. She didn't know about the money his Dad had left him that he hated using. She wasn't after money. She was the girl who just suddenly showed up and wanted to spend time with him this afternoon. It was so great to be with someone who just wanted to be with you.

Chapter 7

Kaye returned to work the next day to a class full of kids disappointed because the weather forecast had predicted snow, but the skies had not delivered enough of the fluffy white stuff to have school cancelled. Upon returning from lunch she checked her mailbox to find a note from the secretary asking her to call a Mr. Carl Brown. She knew this had to be Cammy Jo's father and made a point to call him during her planning period. He asked for an appointment to see her and she scheduled for him to come the next morning before school started. That was the time that would be less of an interference with Mr. Brown's work hours and Kaye didn't mind coming in a little early.

Kaye stopped by Mrs. Adam's office to tell her about the appointment. Mrs. Adams asked that Kaye keep her apprised of what went on during the conference since the Cabinet of Human Resources had an open case on the Brown children. A social worker from the Division of Child Protective Services had called Counselor Adams earlier that morning to confirm that the children had been enrolled and were attending school at Hope Springs.

"Do you know why they have an open case?" Kaye asked.

"You know how they are, Kaye. All they can tell us is that there is an open case. They're never allowed to give us very many details. It's frustrating," Mrs. Adams informed her.

"No, I didn't know that all they could tell us was they had an open case," Kaye returned. "How is that supposed to help us deal with these kids? It most certainly is frustrating! If we knew a little more, maybe we could be a bit more helpful."

"Perhaps, but that's how it is for now, and I don't think you and I are going to be able to change that any time soon."

"I guess, not, Mrs. Adams. I'll let you know what Mr. Brown wants after I see him tomorrow morning."

"Okay, Kaye. Thanks."

The next morning Kaye was very surprised to see a very well dressed man come into her classroom toting a backpack and introduce himself as Carl Brown.

"Hello, Miss Mason. I'm Carl Brown and I need to get Cammy Jo's backpack to her. I'm sure she needs her school supplies. I picked them up from her last school. Please look at them and see if there's anything else she might need and I'll get it here before school starts tomorrow."

Kaye thought, *Sometimes this job is just amazing. Cammy Jo's mom shows up in combat boots and here's her father in expensive clothes, bringing in a backpack with supplies in it that he has retrieved from Cammy Jo's former school. Why didn't the mama bring those with her? Obviously Mr. Brown is not lacking financially. Sometimes you feel like someone has just hit you in the forehead with a baseball bat and you've got to get your brain to settle down so you can make some sense out of what's happening around you.*

Blinking and trying to seem composed, Kaye said, "Thank you, Mr. Brown. I'll see that Cammy Jo gets this."

"Will she be here in a few minutes? I'd like to give it to her myself, and see her for a few minutes, if that's all right."

"I suppose it is, Mr. Brown. I can't think of a reason why you shouldn't see your own daughter. I mean there isn't any reason why you shouldn't, is there?" Kaye inquired with raised eyebrows.

"None other than her mother wouldn't like it."

"Oh, I see. Why would she object?"

"It's a long story and I'm not sure I even understand it, Miss Mason. I can't really explain it. She just up and left with my children, and I just happened to hear they were enrolled here from someone in my church who saw them and knew the children were mine."

Kaye couldn't think of anything else to say, so Mr. Brown finally broke the uncomfortable silence and added, "I just want you to know that I care very much for my children and if there's anything they need, you should feel free to contact me. I want to leave my phone number for you."

"That's kind of you, Mr. Brown. I can't think of anything Cammy Jo needs right now. But I will examine the backpack if you'll give it to me. Then I can tell if there's something she needs that isn't in it."

Mr. Brown reluctantly handed Kaye the backpack. Kaye removed a small stuffed animal from the top. "Well, she won't need this for school."

"No, but she always needed it to go to sleep at home. I'd like to see that she gets it."

"You can, Mr. Brown. The buses should be unloading right now."

"Good. Remember to contact me if Cammy Jo needs anything," Mr. Brown reminded Kaye as he handed her a card with his phone number written upon it. Then he took the backpack, shook Kaye's hand and stepped out into the hallway.

Kaye decided she would stand in her doorway and greet her students as they came in that morning. She didn't want to be nosey, but she really felt like she needed to see Cammy Jo's reaction to seeing her father.

When Mr. Brown saw Cammy Jo, he knelt down so he'd be on her level. It seemed like an awkward moment for both Cammy Jo and her father. Cammy Jo smiled when she saw him, but it was a tentative smile accompanied by a quick look at Kaye. A look that almost asked, "Is this all right?" Kaye gave a quick smile back hoping it conveyed some form of reassurance, and then continued saying "Good morning" about twenty more times as her students filed into her room. Kaye saw a glint of tears in Mr. Brown' eyes as he turned and walked away.

How torn everyone in this family is right now. Kids are like rubber bands being pulled this way and that, Kaye thought. *But the result of a stretched rubber band is that it pops back in place right where it was before with a sting. It hurts!*

Kaye hated the thought of Cammy hurting. She made a vow to make absolutely sure that she and Tom were going to last forever before she allowed herself to become pregnant. She was <u>not</u> going to put a child of hers through the pains of a divorce.

Now she had to return to her classroom and somehow wrap her thoughts around how to teach academic essentials to twenty-four, sometimes less than eager, little minds. She knew a little about Cammy's problems and a lot about Cory's and she had to marvel that they had enough ability to concentrate on anything containing 'the three Rs' and absorb it.

Then she realized that her classroom might be the only source of peace or little corner of happiness that existed in a lot of her students' lives. She picked up her chin, put on a smile, and walked through her classroom door determined to make that classroom the place where children wanted to be.

Later that day the attendance clerk walked into Kaye's classroom carrying a student file folder. Kaye was busy using her planning period to record grades from a previous day's assignment while the students were away for music class.

Abby handed the file folder to Kaye and Kaye immediately sensed unease in Abby's attitude. "What's wrong? You look concerned."

"I am, Kaye. It took a while to get all these folders and records from the other schools, but that's not the reason I'm stressed. Open that folder, Kaye. It's Cammy Jo Brown's folder from her previous school. Look at where that child lived before she came here." Kaye did as instructed and then Abby added, "That is one of the most high-end subdivisions in this county. The homes there are expensive. I don't understand it, Kaye. There has to be quite a story behind the reason a woman would leave an environment like that with little kids and place them out in that old hollow with the characters she's living with."

Kaye didn't know what to say. She just looked at the attendance clerk with the puzzle of this situation getting bigger all the time.

Then Abby added, "I noticed Mr. Brown signed in at the office this morning with the purpose of a conference with you. I don't mean to be nosey, Kaye, but he was clean, well-dressed, nicely spoken. I mean, did he convey any other message to you? Do we have a well-dressed abusive monster on our hands, or a mom in combat boots who is off her rocker, or both or what?"

"I don't know, Abby. Mr. Brown seemed nice enough. He brought Cammy Jo her backpack loaded with supplies. He even had her toy stuffed animal in it. Said she used it to sleep."

"Oh, well, Kaye! People! The Lord must look down here and wonder why he didn't just leave it alone after he created all the animals. Sometimes he has to ask himself why he made those last two creatures."

"Well, Abby, Adam and Eve certainly had their share of problems and I guess the problems haven't stopped since."

"Guess not. I know you were busy when I walked in here, so I'll get out of your way and quit bothering you."

"You're never a bother, Abby. Keep me apprised if you learn anymore."

"I will, Kaye. Have a good day," and with that Abby left bearing an armload of folders on new students to be delivered to other teachers. Kaye just hoped the attendance clerk wasn't carrying an armload of problems in addition to the ones she had. She knew, however, that students who moved around a lot could possess lots of needs and problems.

She opened Cammy Jo's folder to look at the informational transfer sheet that teachers were required to forward to the next school where a student enrolled. It said just what Kaye expected: Cammy Jo was a delight to have in class, well behaved, eager to learn, and seemed to be gifted in art.

Oh what a shame we don't have art teachers in our elementary schools, Kaye thought. *I wonder how many talents in our students go untapped because of our lack of expertise?*

She made a note to do some extra research into age appropriate art projects. She'd do her best to let Cammy Jo's creativeness have every outlet possible.

Suddenly she looked at the clock and jumped from her chair. She would maybe make it to pick up her students on time from music class, if she hurried.

While scurrying down the hall, it occurred to her that if Marty was still around she could probably tell her exactly what to do to help Cammy Jo develop her art skills. She wasn't sure, however, that she wanted Marty real close by. If she remembered correctly, Marty was very attractive and a person who was liked by most everyone she met. Kaye remembered that Marty and Tom had visited her Grandpa last spring when he was in the hospital with bypass surgery and that Marty had made Grandpa a special card just for him. Grandpa liked Marty a lot. Tom had to like her a lot too, to keep her paintings for her. Kaye was fighting the jealously thing, but she decided she could do her own research and leave Marty out of it.

The day continued without any further concerns until dismissal time. Cammy Jo's bus was the last to arrive and she was the last child to leave Kaye's classroom.

Kaye looked at Cammy Jo's desk and said, "Wait, Cammy Jo! Aren't you going to take your backpack with you?"

"I pinished all my wuk, Myth Mathon. Don't hab any homewuk, so I don't need to take my backpack wif me."

First mental note on Kaye's list that afternoon: *See the speech pathologist right after school.*

"But, Cammy Jo, your stuffed animal is in your backpack and your Daddy said you needed it to sleep. Don't you want to at least take it with you?"

"I'm sweeping purty dood, Myth Mathon. I don't need it anymore."

Kaye was not going to press the issue and decided to say, "Okay, Cammy Jo, goodbye. Go home and play. You worked hard today."

"I will, Myth Mathon. Doodbye."

Second mental note of the afternoon: *Something is wrong. Why doesn't she want to take that backpack and stuffed animal with her?*

Kaye went over to the backpack. The stuffed animal's head was poking out. So she took the thing out of the bag, studying it for a minute, trying to decide what it was. *Why didn't kids just have nice teddy bears these days,* she thought. *It's probably some creature from a television show.* Then she said out loud, "I'm going to have to start watching some children's shows so I can identify these things." She could tell it had a lot of use, maybe not as much as the stuffed rabbit in storybook, <u>The Velveteen Rabbit</u>, but she wondered why Cammy Jo was avoiding having it with her.

Mrs. Adams walked in and asked, "How'd it go with Cammy Jo's dad this morning? Everyone is curious about this situation including the attendance clerk."

"Yes, I know. She brought me the student folder earlier today."

"Yeah, I heard. What do you think, Kaye? The cabinet will be here tomorrow to do a check on Cammy Jo and see how things are going."

"I'm unclear on a lot right now, Mrs. Adams. Mr. Brown seemed real nice. He brought Cammy Jo her backpack. It even had this stuffed animal in it," Kaye showed the creature to Mrs. Adams and continued with, "He said she always took it to bed with her at night, that she used it to help her to get to sleep. Then when Cammy Jo left for her bus, she didn't want to take her backpack with her, not even this. Whatever it is." Kaye said holding the stuffed animal up for a closer inspection by Mrs. Adams.

"Kaye, I don't know what the thing is either. All I know to say to you at this point is, looks can be deceiving and things aren't always what they seem. But what I suspect is there's a reason Cammy Jo didn't want to take that backpack and toy home with her. Do you think maybe she didn't want her mama to know daddy had been here?"

"I don't know, Mrs. Adams. I suppose that's a possibility."

Chapter 8

Child Protective Services didn't come to see Cammy Jo the next day. They called to say they had an emergency. That afternoon, the sky clouded up and snowflakes the size of quarters started falling on Hope Springs Elementary. It was impossible to keep the children's attention from the windows so Kaye had everyone to turn their desks toward the windows and started an oral storytelling time.

First, she had them to tell her as many words as they could to describe snow. Then she challenged them to use the words in story-starter phrases. She gave them three choices to use, but encouraged them to come up with their own.

1. This evening when I get home, I am going to _____.
2. If I could do anything in the snow that I wanted to do, I would_____.
3. Snow to me is_____.

She said they could make up a story or write a poem. It didn't have to be very long, but should have at least two things they would do or two things snow meant to them. She would write down what they said and they all could see how many different ways they would write about snow.

When she asked them, Kaye got the usual, expected responses: I'll build a snowman. I am going to build a snow fort and have a snowball fight with my dad.

Then another student added, "Yeah, I am going to make a whole pile of snowballs and let my big brother have it. He tore up my bike and I'm mad at him."

"Not, me," one of the girls said, "I'm gonna make a snow angel and pretend I can fly up to the sky and sit on a cloud."

"Gee, that's nice," Kaye chimed in. "I wonder what snow looks like from up there with you sitting on a cloud watching while it's falling down to the ground."

"You'd have to have an airplane to find out, Miss Mason."

"Or a helicopter," another student added.

Another asked, "Can a helicopter fly in a snow storm?"

"I'm not sure, Nathan. I guess it would depend on how much snow is falling, what the temperatures are and a whole lot of other variables," Kaye answered, knowing many times she didn't have the answers to Nathan's questions. He tended to be a fairly deep thinker for such a young person.

Nathan thought for a minute, then said, "I'm gonna ask my dad. He'll know all about variables."

"Do that, Nathan, and let us know what he says," Kaye suggested.

The last comment about snow came from a small girl named Kelly who read what she wrote; "We always make snow crème at my house when it snows. Snow + Milk + Sugar = Yum!"

"That's great, Kelly. I remember making snow crème with my family when I was a little girl. I still like it. Might make some this afternoon if we get enough snow," Kaye said, concluding the conversations about snow and asking the students to bring her the papers they had written. The trip to her desk would at least let them get out of their seats and expend a little energy. Plus, it was time to tidy up the room, get coats on and be ready to go home.

Cammy Jo had remained quiet during the exchange about snow, smiling at the things the other students said. Kaye collected the papers and shuffled them a bit so she could read what Cammy Jo wrote.

Her paper said: Snow falling, blowing, coming in my window, cold and wet, making my pink blanket white.

At first, Kaye thought this was beautifully poetic. Then considered it much too poetic for a child to write. She wondered if the child had actually experienced what she had written.

The classroom erupted in a scurry to get coats from lockers, to get all buttons buttoned, and zippers zipped because Kaye said she wouldn't let them out the door until those things were accomplished. They settled into their desks waiting for afternoon announcements, which told them to be sure and listen to the news the next morning to learn if school would take place or be cancelled.

Kaye was a little worried for the bus drivers as the ground had already accumulated enough snow to turn it white. She knew, however, that the kids going home on buses were safer than those being picked up by parents in cars. The buses were a lot heavier and much less likely to slip off the road. Most of her students were bus riders so she wasn't too worried about their safety. Not wanting to delay her afternoon drive and cause herself to be in any unnecessary danger with the snow accumulating as fast as it was, she quickly gathered up papers to grade and books to plan lessons. But she noticed before she left that the stuffed animal was missing from Cammy Jo's backpack.

Grandma Katie gathered up the last of the supper dishes from the dining room. She found Kaye in the kitchen with her books and papers spread out all over the kitchen table. "I remember when Bill and Bob used to do their homework at this table. Don't guess you can call what you're doing homework though."

"Oh, I don't know, Grandma. I think the teacher has more homework than the kids. You should have seen them when the snow started falling today. I couldn't keep their attention for anything."

"What do you do when that happens? Must be hard to teach."

"It is. You get inventive. I gave up on social studies and had them make up stories about snow. They talked and they wrote. I'm reading some of their stories now. Take a look."

"Gracious, Kaye, this one's going to clobber his brother with snowballs. Oh, yes, snow angels and snow crème. The way it's coming down, we'll have to make some."

"Make some what?" Grandpa Roth questioned as he enter the back kitchen door, shaking off snow and stomping his boots. Mark Elliott followed Roth in stomping and shaking off snow in an effort not to mess up Miz Katie's kitchen.

"Make some snow crème," Katie answered.

"Oh, wow! My mom used to do that for us kids when we were little," Mark reminisced.

"Won't have to be on the lookout for yellow snow these days, Katie. Bill and Bob aren't around anymore," Roth added with a chuckle

"What?" Kaye asked.

"It's evident that you didn't grow up around any brothers, Kaye. Bill and Bob used to see who could write their names the neatest while peeing in the snow. Your grandmother had to be careful about where she gathered snow for snow crème."

"Oh, my gosh, Grandpa! Now I won't be able to eat any without thinking about that," Kaye said frowning and waving her hand in front of her face.

"Miz Katie, scoop it off the top. I've heard the first snowflakes that fall clear the air of pollution, so you don't want to dig down too deeply to get your snow for snow crème," Mark added.

Katie returned with, "Good grief! Are you two going to completely ruin a good thing? Kaye, Roth's got us dying from urine poisoning and Mark will have us glowing in the dark from some kind of radioactive air pollution. I swear! Have you ever heard the like?"

Kaye just looked at everybody and shook her head. Grandma Katie put the student's paper she'd been reading on the bottom of the stack and Cammy Jo's paper appeared next.

"Kaye, what's this about snow turning a pink blanket white?"

"I am not sure, Grandma. It's beautifully written, but I'm not sure an eight-year-old has the mental capacity to write poetically like that appears to be written."

"Do you think this has happened to her and that's why she can write this?"

"I don't know. What do you think, Grandpa?" Kaye asked handing the paper to her Grandpa. "This is the kid I told you about that you said was living with some real characters back at the end of some hollow. I don't remember what you said the hollow was called."

"It's called Buzzard Hollow, Kaye. It was named that because it is on the same road as the distillery and we all always joked about the buzzards in the sky getting so drunk they can't fly. Like the song says about them smelling that good ole mountain dew. Hard to say what I think about this little girl, Kaye, because I don't really know what I think right now. Hope you're not too worried. Besides, what could any of us do about the situation anyway? Are the child protection people aware of this?"

"Yes, Grandpa. I was told they have an open case. That's all they're allowed to tell us."

"Okay. That's their job. Your job is to teach. Theirs is to handle this kind of thing. I know that's hard, Kaye. I can see that you love this child. But there's a limit to what you're allowed to do."

"I know you're right, Grandpa, but it somehow can't stop me from being concerned."

"You shouldn't stop being concerned. The kid is yours for six hours a day. Just be sensible about what you can and cannot do. You could make yourself sick with worry and that won't do that kid a bit of good. Plus, you have your other students to think about, and from what I hear, some of them have some pretty good problems, too."

"That's true, Grandpa."

"Don't wanna minimize the importance of your concerns here, Kaye, but I brought Mark in here on purpose. Katie, this concerns you," Roth informed her.

"Me? Forevermore! What is this all about?" Katie inquired looking at Mark.

"Well, Miz Katie, I just got a nine-year-old mare in my barn. She is very elegant and looks good pulling a buggy. You can tell that she loves doing it. Looks like she was born to it. What I was wondering is if you would be interested in driving her during next spring and summer's show season?" Mark informed and asked Katie.

"Oh, Grandma! That's wonderful. You're going to do it aren't you?" Kaye broke in clapping her hands excitedly.

"You'd really enjoy her, Miz Katie, and you'd be perfect. I know you can handle her." Mark added.

Roth had leaned against the kitchen counter, one leg crossed in front of the other with his arms crossed over his chest, watching the reactions and finally looking at Katie and grinning.

"Oh, I don't know, Mark. I'm too old for all that," Katie replied looking back at Roth who continued to smile at her.

"Grandma, you are not!" Kaye quickly countered.

"It's only February. You'd have March and April to practice with the mare before any serious shows took place in May. I'll give you as much training time as you need," Mark offered.

"Oh, this is plum silly you all," Katie returned. "Surely you can't be serious about this, Roth," Katie said, looking at her husband and shaking her head from side to side.

"Katie, I haven't seen the mare. Mark was just talking to me about her in the barn after supper and suggested that we talk to you about driving her. We know Mark well enough to know he's not going to put you with an animal that's likely to hurt you," Roth returned. "Plus, I think it would be good for you. This house is clean enough and I certainly eat enough. Why don't you get out of here and go do something else for a change. Go have some fun. You've spent the last year playing nursemaid to me after the operation and your whole life has been spent taking care of this family. You need to go do something for Katie once in a while."

"Grandpa's right, Grandma. Go for it!" Kaye enthusiastically encouraged her grandmother.

Katie was speechless, not knowing quite how to respond. It seemed like someone had picked her up off the ground and left her dangling there and wouldn't put her back down. She just couldn't for the life of her think how to respond appropriately to this ridiculous notion.

"Miz Katie, tell you what, before you restrict yourself with the idea that you shouldn't or you can't do this, come over to my stable, drive the horse in my indoor arena, and see what you think," Mark plied.

Katie came back with, "What I think?! Why, what's everyone else going to think about an old woman in her seventies driving a horse around?"

"They used to do it all the time, Grandma. How else would they get around?" Kaye added.

"That was then. This is now. I don't have to drive a team of horses to go someplace. I can still drive a car, you know," Katie was beginning to sound defensive and that's when Roth decided to step in.

"Yep. You drive that old car just fine, Katie, my darling, and I bet you can still drive a horse just as well. Let's go over to Mark's barn tomorrow. Mark can drive the mare first. You can see what you think and if you don't want to drive her, you certainly don't have to."

"Can we sleep on this tonight and let me decide in the morning?" Katie requested.

"Sure can. No decision has to be made at this moment, Miz Katie," Mark assured her.

"I'll call you in the morning and let you know what she decides, Mark," Roth assured him.

"Good. You folks have a good night." With that Mark turned and went back out the door, saying, "I better get going. This snow isn't letting up."

Chapter 9

Katie was up before anyone the next morning, as usual, fixing coffee and planning breakfast. Enough snow had fallen that by the time the eleven o'clock news was broadcast the night before, school had already been called off.

Kaye had announced that she wasn't going to set her alarm so she could sleep in and Roth hadn't come alive yet, so, Katie had the kitchen all to herself. The small television she had placed on the countertop had weathermen predicting falling temperatures throughout the day.

Local schools had snowplows clearing parking lots and state and county road crews were busy clearing highways. So far no fatalities had occurred like they had with the last snowfall. This time the snow had not been preceded with freezing rain that turns to black ice on the highways. Katie remembered how worried she had been about Kaye being stranded in Lexington and then having to make it home after that storm let up at the end of December.

Then her thoughts turned to the proposal that Mark had made that she drive a horse and buggy in the upcoming horse show season during the spring and summer. Surely Mark had a customer who would lease that horse for the season or perhaps even buy it. If the mare really was that nice, why wasn't he making this offer to a client who would be willing to pay him good money for this opportunity? She and Roth let Mark use their horse barn and outdoor riding arena during the summer months and some stalls during the winter and didn't charge him very much. Maybe he thought he owed them some sort of a favor and that was why he was offering to let Katie show the mare. To Katie's way of thinking, he was doing enough already by training the young filly they called Honey.

Oh, my, she thought, *what if the cart turns over. I could be hurt and hurt the horse. I don't mend as easily as I once did.*

She heard footsteps that she recognized as Roth's. He came in the kitchen at the same time the weather forecaster was telling everyone to expect a bitterly cold night. Roth watched then said, "Well, if it gets that cold, Kaye will have another day off. They won't put kids out in weather that cold to go to school. Plus, half the buses probably won't even start in temperatures like that. Hot coffee! Good! Woman, you are after my heart."

Katie smiled and said, "I thought I already had your heart."

He laughed, patted her on the rump and assured her, "You do! Have since the moment I laid eyes on you. Don't guess we'll go to Mark's today. Roads won't be cleared. It'll be too dangerous and unless the temperature comes up tomorrow, we'll have to put it off another day. Don't want to work a horse in temperatures that cold or have you out in it either. Not good for you or the horse."

Katie only smiled but thought, *Good! Maybe I can come up with some reasons why not to do this if I'm given a couple of days. Weddings, horseshows, this is all too much to deal with for an old gal.*

When Kaye woke up, she went in search of Grandma Katie and found her in the laundry room folding clothes. "You know, Kaye, I always wanted to expand this room to include a craft area."

"That would be a nice thing for you Grandma," Kaye agreed, looking around the room that presently had space for a washer, dryer, ironing board and a long table where Katie folded clothes. "Why didn't you call me? I could have helped you fold," Kaye scolded. "I sometimes feel I'm taking advantage of being here with you when you don't ask me to help."

"Oh, Kaye, it wasn't nothing but a bunch of old towels. I didn't need any help. Look, if we took out this wall, I could make the room big enough to leave my sewing machine set up all the time. Then we could put a door at the end with a little sitting area outside where I could do the messy part of cleaning my gourds," Katie proceeded, entirely absorbed in the remodeling ideas. "I'd need big windows down there so I could see better how to paint and carve. With a small table and an electrical outlet, I could even do a lot of my carving outside. Then I wouldn't need to run extension cords. That would eliminate all that gourd dust from being in the house. I certainly don't want gourd flu."

"Gourd flu? Are you serious, Grandma? Is there really such a thing as gourd flu?"

"Sure is, and it can make you quite sick from what I've heard. I try to always wear a mask when I'm doing things to the gourds that creates dust."

Katie belonged to the local gourd society and had been a member for years. She never competed in the annual show, but gave the gourds away to auctions for charitable causes and to friends and family as presents.

"The room sounds good, Grandma. Do you have a birthday, anniversary or something coming up soon so we could ask Grandpa to build your craft room?" Kaye wanted to know.

"He's in no shape to be taking on a project like that right now, Kaye. But speaking of anniversaries, have you and Tom settled on a date yet? You're never gonna have an anniversary if you don't get married first."

"No. Tom's left that up to you, Mom and me. I thought we'd settle on a date when Mom and Dad come back in on President's Day. That's when we are supposed to finalize everything. We'll have plenty of time after that weekend to get invitations printed and do all the other things needed. I'll have three days off. Hey, remember the something borrowed, something blue? Mom's doing the blue. You said you had the something borrowed," Kaye reiterated.

"Yes, I do," Katie confirmed. "Let's go up into the attic. We'll get in your great grandmother's trunk and let's see if what I have is something you want to borrow."

Roth pulled the attic ladder down and cautioned both ladies to take care going up and to be extra careful coming down. "Too many people depend on both of you for you to get hurt," he admonished.

Katie climbed up, found the trunk she wanted, opened it and removed an oblong box. Kaye was trying to imagine what was in it and when Katie took the lid off, Kaye screamed with delight. "Oh, Grandma! I can't believe this! It's so beautiful!"

Kaye was so loud that Roth rushed to the bottom of the steps and yelled up, "Are you two all right?"

"Yes, Grandpa. Sorry. We're fine. I'm just a little too excited is all."

Roth returned to his seat in the living room grumbling, "Scare an old man to death!"

"Grandma, was this really your mother's?" Kaye asked, holding up a very delicate and beautiful bridal veil.

"Yes, Kaye. It was."

"Is this what I can borrow?"

"If you want to wear it, yes."

"If I want to wear it? Are you kidding? Look at these little tiny pearls in the headband. They're gorgeous."

"They're just buttons, Kaye, not real pearls."

"Yes, but they are still gorgeous," Kaye observed, while she carefully laid the veil back in the box. Then she reached across it and hugged her grandmother. She spied a hatbox at the end of the trunk and asked, "Is that a hat, Grandma?"

"It's just a derby I used to wear back when we showed our horses."

"I want to see it. Is it all right?"

"Go ahead. It's nothing but a navy blue derby."

Kaye opened the box and admired the hat. It was in perfect condition. "Where's the rest of your outfit, Grandma? I bet you were smashing in it."

"Oh, I sold all those things when I quit riding, everything but the derby. I figured somebody else could get some use out of them. No need to keep 'em around when I wasn't going to be using 'em."

Kaye started to put the derby back in the box, but noticed that there were pictures underneath where the hat had been. She handed the hat to her Grandma, removed the pictures and started leafing through them. They were pictures of Katie in her riding habits, showing Lady Red and two other horses.

"Grandma, these are lovely. I was right! You were smashing in your riding clothes. I recognize Lady Red. Is this Sugar that you are driving?"

"Yes. We used to show Saddlebreds and Tennessee Walkers at the same shows years ago. They are not shown together very much anymore. After we retired Lady Red, we just concentrated on Saddlebreds. I really enjoyed my Tennessee Walker, however, so we kept Lady Red and I rode her around here on trails just for fun. But I think she misses the show ring," Katie admitted, looking at Red in one of the old pictures Kaye handed to her.

"Don't you miss it, too, Grandma? Look how nice you look driving Sugar. You should take Mark up on his offer."

"*Looked*, Kaye, that's the word, *looked*. How nice I *looked*, not *look*. That picture was taken, at what seems like to me, ages ago," Katie reminded Kaye.

Kaye wasn't going to give up that easily. Her grandmother was a delightful person and still very attractive. She had a warm inner glow and even though Grandma Katie ignored it, Kaye couldn't help but see what a commanding presence her grandmother still had. She could walk through the grocery store and still get admiring looks from everyone, not just older men. People went out of their way to speak to her and to hold doors open for her. Kaye speculated that Grandma Katie probably thought this was only because she was old. *Old*, Kaye thought. *It really is a frame of mind.* She had trouble thinking of her grandma as old. She was way too active to be thought of as old.

Kaye knew that anyone beyond thirty was considered old to a little kid. When did old stop seeming to be old in an adult's mind? Maybe it occurred when you wanted to deny seeing someone age while you witnessed their birthdays float by. She thought, *This is probably because of the fear of losing someone close to you.* Then her additional thought was, *Maybe it occurred when you wanted to overlook the symptoms in yourself.* She'd heard so many times people saying, "My mind doesn't think *old*, but my body says otherwise."

"Grandma, you'd be a little nervous but you'd get over it, and then you would have a ball at some of the smaller horse shows at our county fairs this summer. I'm sure Mark wasn't considering putting you up against high priced horses and drivers at big shows like Rock Creek and Lexington Junior League."

"I know he wouldn't. Because I'm not stupid enough to even attempt to compete on that kind of a level." Katie confirmed. "Let's take the veil downstairs and get it in a better light so we can do a thorough inspection of it. Then we can be sure you can use it and have your 'something borrowed'." Katie closed the trunk and Kaye put the pictures and the hat back in the box. Kaye was truly hoping she'd get to see her grandmother flying around a show ring with a beautiful horse in front of her next summer. It would be so much fun!

The two women descended the stairs and Roth came to assist with folding up the steps on the attic ladder and sealing away all the past that was stored up there. Katie told him, "I'm going to have to spend a day up there, Roth, and get rid of some old junk."

"Maybe you ought to get rid of some of the cobwebs, too," Roth added, picking one out of Katie's hair.

"That, too," Katie added.

"I want to help," Kaye offered. "I discover wonderful surprises plus, I get to learn so much from the things that we uncover up there. Look at this veil, Grandpa. Isn't it lovely? It was great grandma's," Katie said, opening the box to show Roth her ancient treasure.

"Looks a lot like what they wear today, doesn't it?" Roth added.

"Sure does," Kaye came back, touching the veil in different places as she held it up and turned it around. "You know what else I saw while I was up there, Grandpa?"

"Tell me."

"I found Grandma's hatbox with her derby in it and pictures of her riding Lady Red and driving Sugar. She looked great!"

"Always did. Still would if this horse works out with Mark. I just talked to him on the phone and we agreed to wait a couple of days until Saturday to go see the mare. Too much snow on the road to travel safely today and with the temperatures plummeting like they say they're going to tonight, it's probably not going to warm up much tomorrow. So, we agreed to wait until Saturday. Hope that's okay, Katie."

"It's fine with me. I think it's silly to even be considering this at all," Katie pursed her lips and glared at Roth as she spoke.

"Now, Katie, you never know. You might have a chance at driving another Be Happy," Roth countered.

"Oh, yeah, right Roth. Be sensible! If that horse Mark has was another Be Happy, she would not be available for me to drive. She'd be in a big stable somewhere and a professional trainer would be driving while someone with more money than sense watched from the sidelines, yelling, 'That's my horse!'" Katie countered right back.

Kaye chose to ignore Grandma Katie's discomfort, and said, "If you go Saturday, I can go with you. I won't be working. I can't wait."

"I think I can!" Katie said shaking her head. With that, she went back to her laundry room and, tapping her fingers on her chin, contemplated what it would take to knock out that back wall and make her craft room. *Makes more sense than trying to drive a horse,* she thought.

Chapter 10

Sure enough, temperatures were dropping to dangerously cold levels that evening and Tom was busy plugging in heating tapes to prevent water lines from freezing in his old house. He had talked to Kaye on the phone earlier and they had agreed to spend Friday together if school was called off. Most of the roads were clear, and the air temperature had risen to a level during the day so that snow had melted off of the road surfaces, leaving most roads fairly dry. So, even with the low temperatures during the night, it wasn't likely that the roads would ice over, but caution was still the word-of-the-day. Tom told Kaye he'd come and get her in his four-wheel-drive truck. He didn't want her out on snowy roads in her compact car, not even roads that had been cleared.

Morning brought a frosty bite to the air, but no water pipes had burst and Tom felt real proud of his plumbing work. He settled down to a steamy bowl of oatmeal and a cup of hot coffee with thoughts of what he and Kaye could do that day.

He thought about renting some movies she might like to watch. They could ride into town and select some. He thought he'd better let her select them. He wasn't real good at selecting chick flicks. They could compromise, one chick flick for her and one that he'd like to watch. He wasn't real up on movies lately either and had no idea what he wanted to see. He'd wait until he got to the store and then make a selection. He just hoped she didn't want to see <u>Dr. Shivago</u>. That was one chick flick he was familiar with. It was cold enough today without watching that sled running through Russia in snow ass-deep to a giraffe, only to arrive at a damn ice palace. He never did believe those people were able to thaw out, even if they did build a fire as big as Texas in that huge fireplace that was large enough that you could walk into it.

The phone rang with Kaye at the other end. "Hey, you didn't sleep in today. Figured you would with school cancelled and all," Tom observed.

"Nope. Too excited about spending the day with you."

"I have to feed some animals, check on livestock, and then I'll be over to get you."

"Okay. I'll be right here."

"See that you are. I don't want you out on the roads yet in your little car. I worried too much the last time."

"Don't worry. I'm not going anywhere until you get here. What are we going to do today?"

"I thought we could watch some movies and pop some more popcorn."

"Sounds great! See you in a little while. Listen, Grandpa has the Lonesome Dove series. Would you like to see that?"

"Sure, then we won't have to drive into town to get movies. That is unless there's something else you want to see."

"No, Lonesome Dove is fine,"

"Okay, see you in a bit." Tom hung up the phone thinking what a joy Kaye was to suggest seeing a series about old cowboys moving cattle. Of course, there was romance in those movies, too, if you could call it that. He liked to think that what he and Kaye shared was a lot greater than what all those lonesome cowboys had. He was sure of it. Maybe that was why those cowboys were so lonesome and all he had to do was think about Kaye and his lonesome feelings disappeared.

Chapter 11

Saturday brought an elevation in the temperatures. It was enough of a break in the weather for Roth to feel that Katie could endure the temperatures in Mark's barn. So he, Katie and Kaye drove over to take a look at the mare Mark wanted Katie to drive.

Mark purposefully had Miguel, his stable hand, to pull the buggy out into the arena so he could bring Kentucky's Secret Premier out and drive her on lines before hooking her to the buggy.

When Secret stepped into the arena, all three observers took a large, through-the-mouth, intake of breath. They laughed at each other for the gasp they had simultaneously made.

The horse was beautiful. "What's her name, Mark?" Katie asked.

"Kentucky's Secret Premier. We call her Secret."

Katie couldn't help it. She really had intended to play the role of being unimpressed, but instead she said, "Well, she's certainly been a well-kept secret. Who's been hiding her? Does she work as good as she looks?"

"Another barn needed some beginning lesson horses, Miz Katie. You know how hard it is to find good horses for beginners. I had some I could let go, and he didn't want to do it, but he let me have this horse in exchange. I don't have a lot of students who are beginning riders right now. If I did, I'd have to hire another instructor. Most of my riding students are beyond the beginner stage, and I am working hard to keep all their horses in full training and give them their lessons. So, we did a temporary exchange. He'll use the lesson horses until his students step up to more advanced horses and then, I'll get my horses back and he'll take this horse back. So Secret's here on a temporary basis."

"Yes, Mark, but shouldn't you use her to make some money? Surely you have clients who are ready to use this horse," Katie questioned.

"I do, Miz Katie. There's a younger kid, a boy who likes driving. He'd be in a different showing division than you, and I think Secret can handle both of you. Well, I'll correct myself. I know she can handle you and Michael. No problem. He has already driven her and loves her. I really want to keep Michael interested. You know we don't get a lot of boys around a Saddlebred barn and Michael is showing some real promise toward making a good horseman. So let's hook her up and see what you think."

Miguel started assisting with the buggy as Mark had Secret step into the shafts. The horse was a beautiful light chestnut color with a flaxen mane and tail, the kind of horse that would really get noticed in the ring. She was certain to catch everyone's eye.

Mark took Secret around the indoor arena about four times before reversing her and taking her the other way. While Katie was watching, she turned to Kaye and Roth and said, "Well, I hope this Michael kid doesn't get too attached to this horse. If she's friendly in the stall and he shows her successfully all summer, he'll have a broken heart when he has to give her up when she has to go back to the other barn."

Roth winked at Kaye and asked Katie, "Does that mean that you're already in love?"

"I didn't say that, Roth, but you and I can already see that she's just what Mark said: a beautiful horse. She's plenty game in harness, too."

"Yes, I can see all that Katie."

Kaye had maintained silence through all the exchange between her grandparents, but had the feeling this show season was going to be twice the fun as last summer's season had been.

It would be great watching Grandma Katie show this horse. She couldn't imagine that her grandmother wasn't at least going to give this a try.

Mark brought Secret to the center of the ring and dismounted from the buggy. "Want to give her a try, Kaye?"

"Are you kidding? I'd love to, but shouldn't Grandma be doing that?"

Katie immediately said, "You go ahead, Kaye. I don't mind watching some more." That was exactly what Mark wanted. He wanted Katie to see that almost anyone with any experience at all could drive this horse.

Kaye took two turns each way and then brought Secret in again to the center of the ring. She parked out beautifully, even in harness. "Your turn, Grandma," Kaye announced.

"Well, I guess I'm going to have to give this a try," Katie replied.

Driving that mare was such a feeling. Old age seemed to fly right out the barn roof. The exhilaration was something Katie hadn't felt in a long time. The endless worry about Roth's health seemed lifted right off her shoulders, and before she parked the mare, Katie's thoughts were already turning to planning the outfit she would wear to the shows.

Another plus was, she wouldn't have to handle the horse on the ground a lot, because grooming and hooking her up would be the job of Mark and his staff. Katie knew she was going to have a last hurrah this summer. If she acted like she had any sense at all in the stall, she was going to show this horse.

Mark held the horse's bridle just as a safety precaution while Roth assisted Katie from the buggy. "Thanks, Roth, but you know I'll need to get in and out of the buggy on my own if I'm going to do this."

With that, Roth stepped away and said, "Okay, go for it."

Katie swung her legs over the side of the buggy landing with a little bounce that said, 'I can do it myself.' Kaye watched everything with a smile.

Miguel came to assist with unhooking Secret from the buggy. He and Mark had already agreed to take the harness off in the arena, put a halter on Secret, and hand the lead line to Katie.

When he did, Katie said, "Oh, ho! You really know how to make a sale don't you, Mark."

"Sure do. That's how I make a living, Miz Katie. Take her back to stall number five. Kaye can show you where it is."

Miguel followed, loaded down with harness while Mark and Roth conferred. Miguel just smiled. He knew Mark hadn't really made the sale. The mare had sold herself. He put the harness away and took a grooming box to Secret's stall.

Katie was petting the horse, running her hands down her legs, picking up her feet and speaking gently to Secret when Miguel arrived at the stall. "Oh, let me get out of your way," Katie said starting to exit the stall."

"No, you do it," Miguel said, handing Katie the brush. "I plug in the drier so she can get dry. She not afraid."

Katie looked at Kaye and said, "They're working hard at this."

Miguel overheard and said, "Don't have to. She's beautiful horse, nice mannered, too."

Katie continued brushing and smiled. She was enjoying Miguel's broken English almost as much as she was enjoying the horse. Secret didn't move at the sound of the hair dryer or at the feeling of the warm air blowing on her.

Katie agreed to start out with two lessons per week. She'd come in the mornings after breakfast.

Roth knew he was coming too. Mark had brought a lot of pleasure into his life since he'd let the boy lease his horse barn at his old farm. Not only did Roth get to see Honey trained and speculate on seeing her shown, now he'd get to enjoy seeing his Katie having fun showing this beautiful horse named Secret.

He was considering not charging Mark a thing to lease his barn and arena. He didn't really need the money and the pleasure he was deriving from his association with Mark was worth more than money. He could offer to pay Mark for the time he spent with Katie and the horse she was going to drive, but it seemed kind of silly. Mark would be giving him money to lease the barn and he would be turning right around and giving it back to him for Katie's lessons. He'd just tell Mark they would call it even and not be handing money back and forth.

When they got back home and Kaye was out of earshot, he said to Katie. "Wonder how long before Tom and Kaye will give us some great-grandkids? Our filly, Honey, and the kids could grow up together and show together."

"Roth, there's no guarantee great-grandkids would even have an interest in showing horses," Katie said, shaking her head at all of Roth's future planning for kids that hadn't even arrived yet.

"Yes, they will," Roth returned, "It's in their blood."

"Their blood?" Katie came back. "They don't even have any blood yet. They're not even born."

"Yes, they do. They have plenty of blood, right here and now. Good Blood! And they <u>will</u> be here, real soon. You'll see."

Katie just smiled and hugged her very optimistic husband. Boy, she was glad she didn't have one of those miserable old gripers she heard so many women her age complaining about having to live with daily.

Chapter 12

Monday meant a return to the routine of work on the farm for Tom and to the routine of teaching for Kaye. For Kaye, however, Monday proved to be anything but routine. School was back in session with a bang. She wondered what parents fed children while they were away from the classroom to make them so antsy.

The noise level stayed elevated all morning. Clayton was attracting the attention of the majority of his classmates by moon walking to the pencil sharpener, which set off a rash of needs in the other students to sharpen their pencils. Only sharpening meant grinding the wooden sticks down until they were no longer usable. Then there were the complaints of "Miss Mason, I don't have a pencil. I can't finish my work."

This resulted in a class meeting to establish rules of restrictions on the pencil sharpener. Order seemed to be established by the time lunch rolled around.

Kaye stopped by the office to gather her in-house mail to find a note from the receptionist that said, "Please call Cammy Jo's mother" with the phone number listed. *Well, the folks living in the hollow must not be too far behind the times. Seems like they do have a telephone.* A second note said to please prepare for a meeting with Child Protective Services the following day during her planning period. That note was from Counselor Adams.

Planning period, Kaye thought, *I don't think we can call it that anymore. It has become my meeting period. I can see why some of the teachers get so upset over all these meetings. I don't have a lot of demands on my time at home, but if I was married with a house to keep, and a child or two needing my attention, in addition to trying to find time for my husband when I got home, I guess I'd get upset, too. All these meetings shift all the lesson planning and grading papers you would have done during your planning period, right into your after school hours when you have other things needing your attention.*

Kaye returned Mrs. Brown's call after school. Mrs. Brown asked if she could come in and meet with Kaye for a conference. Kaye scheduled the meeting to take place after school on Wednesday. Then she headed home, glad to be going toward what she hoped was a little bit of sanity.

Tuesday settled into a great day with her students and Kaye said a little prayer of thanks, thinking, *If all days were like yesterday, no one would ever want to teach.*

When time for her planning period rolled around, Kaye ushered her students off to P. E. and a round of bowling training with Mrs. Snyder, the P.E. teacher. Kaye couldn't help wondering if parents and students knew how much to appreciate that lady. She certainly was never exposed to the variety of games and physical activity that this lady provided the students at Hope Springs Elementary.

Kaye arrived at the counselor's office to find a committee of people from Child Protective Services. She was not, evidently, the only one who was so attracted to the Brown children's pleasant ways. The cabinet had been aware of the family for quite a bit longer than Kaye, and found the situation as incongruous as the personnel of the school found it.

No one quite understood why Mrs. Brown had left her husband and had left what the cabinet described as a beautiful home where there was plenty of money to meet a family's needs.

Kaye felt icy cold shock creep up her neck when the younger social worker said, "I had to be restrained from going out there the other night and getting those kids. The window in Cammy Jo's bedroom is broken out and when the temperatures dropped so low, I just panicked. The only thing that stopped me was I knew I'd get arrested and lose my job. I have a family I have to provide for and think of first, or I would have been right out there."

Kaye left that meeting feeling sick. She wanted to take Cammy Jo home with her and take care of her more than ever now. Kaye hurried to pick her students up from their P.E. class. As Cammy Jo passed by Kaye in line, she said, "Dat was fun, Myth Mathon. Cory bolds willy whale." Cammy Jo patted Cory on the back.

"Yeah! All my pins fell down, Miz Mason!" Cory added.

"That's great, Cory. Maybe you'll turn into a professional bowler like the guys on television."

"Naw, I wanna be a football player like my big brother Jason."

"Well, maybe you will, Cory. You have plenty of time to do that yet."

Both kids practically skipped back to the room. Even though walking in the halls was a requirement, Kaye couldn't bring herself to end those two children's moment of merriment. They both deserved some happiness in their lives and Kaye wasn't about to dampen their mood.

Well, I'll meet with Mrs. Brown tomorrow. Wonder what surprises that meeting has in store for me? Kaye wondered.

Kaye passed the counselor's office on her way out that afternoon and Mrs. Adams called out to her to come into her office. "Kaye, I know I'm a counselor certified to counsel elementary age students, but I think I'd better spend a moment or two with you. For a first year teacher, it seems to me that you're getting bombarded with a lot of social problems that students carry into the classroom with them. Thank goodness Cammy Jo and Cory seem, at least to me, to be good, well-behaved students."

"They are, Mrs. Adams. I guess that's what breaks my heart even more. I mean I'm pleased that they are well-behaved, but I have to admit my heart's been in my throat several times this year with thoughts about those two."

"That's why I wanted to talk to you. One of the first things we learn in counseling is to ask ourselves, 'Who owns the problem?' While you are the one who is hearing about it, you do not own the problem. You can help to some degree, but most of the solving has to come from the owner of the problem. A counselor's job is just to point them in the right direction toward being able to make things in their life be, hopefully, a little bit better."

"I guess—no, I know you're right, Mrs. Adams, but it's hard not to worry about those two kids."

"You have a right to worry for a while, but not so long that it spoils your life. Remember, you don't own the problem. Now, Kaye, go home and enjoy your evening. You really don't know that Cammy Jo and Cory aren't enjoying theirs. They may be having loads of fun right now, doing something they want to do."

"Thanks, Mrs. Adams. I guess I needed this."

"After hearing the social worker today, I'm sure you did. By the way, Cory's mom called today, just to check on things. Seems like she's moving full steam ahead with her education plans and really doing a good job of taking care of those boys. She just sounded so much better."

"That's great! I guess sometimes solutions do float to the top, don't they, Mrs. Adams."

"Usually do, Kaye. Now get out of here and go enjoy that fiancé of yours. If I had him on a string, I wouldn't be standing here."

Kaye smiled, turned and walked away, looked at her watch and hurried to her car. She'd have to hustle. It was Tuesday night and near time for her line dance lessons with Tom. She was hoping for a couple of waltzes during the interlude between review of last week's lesson and the start of teaching a new dance. Tonight, she really needed to be held in Tom's arms.

Kaye woke at five fifteen Wednesday morning before anyone else in the house was up. She went carefully down the stairs trying hard not to let them moan in protest. She knew the fourth step from the bottom had a severe case of arthritis and moaned every time it had to bear weight. She clung tightly to the railing and the banisters. That enabled her to skip that step.

She started coffee and sat looking out the kitchen window facing the eastern sky. It was a sky streaked with the orange glow of morning that crept in as the sun peaked over the distant trees. The aroma of the coffee and the quiet calm of the morning in the old house wrapped around Kaye with a coziness equal to one of Grandma Katie's soft baby afghans that she crocheted for all the newborns in the family.

How appropriate that the kitchen was on the east side of the house to receive the morning light and dark at night. But these days the family was bathed in light from the convenience of electric lighting at night. The house was over one hundred years old and Kaye could imagine a time when that light would have come from coal oil lanterns. Grandma Katie had some newer versions that attached to the walls with reflective metal plates behind them. They were back up lighting in case of electrical outages and had come in handy many times throughout the years.

Kaye's thoughts turned to Cammy Jo and she wondered if the child was warm enough this morning. The temperatures weren't bitterly cold, but they were cold enough to require heavy coats, hats and gloves, especially for children standing outside waiting for the bus. What a difference between Cory and Cammy Jo. One in a really nice house, the other in what people described as inadequate for habitat.

One thing was really evident, it doesn't matter what the socioeconomic status, problems could surface in wealth as well as in poverty. Only, for Cammy Jo, it seemed the problems had been there for her in both places.

Then Kaye's thoughts wandered back to the advice the school counselor, Mrs. Adams, had given her. "Ask yourself: Who owns the problem?" Even though she knew Mrs. Adams was a professional and probably had many coping mechanisms, she still wondered how she was able to deal with all the problems that came across her desk. Kaye's class was only one in that school and she knew all the kids with problems had not been assigned to just her classroom. *Must have to be a special kind of person to be a counselor,* Kaye mused. *Not sure I would want to tackle that job.*

Kaye heard a noise and realized that Grandma Katie was coming downstairs. That fourth step from the bottom told on her. "You've made coffee. What a treat! I can't remember when someone else made morning coffee in this house besides me. So what are you doing up so early?"

Kaye lied a little and said, "Don't know. Just woke up." She didn't want her grandma worrying over things neither one of them could not do anything about. So she decided to follow Mrs. Adams advice and not own the problems that weren't hers this morning.

She turned the conversation to what she hoped would be a more pleasant exciting topic. "I didn't get to see much of you last night with my time being spent with Tom at line dancing. How'd the driving session go with Mark?"

Katie turned around with a big smile of pleasure and said, "Great! That horse is just what Mark said she was. She's wonderful."

"I just had to believe she would be, Grandma. I have some extra time this morning. How about I cook breakfast for you for a change."

"My, I'll be spoiled enough to stink if this keeps up. Coffee made for me, then breakfast, and later today, a driving lesson with Secret."

"Sounds like a perfect day to me, Grandma. Go use the bathroom and get those riding clothes on. I know you go early for your riding lesson and I'm going to need the bathroom soon to get ready for work. Your breakfast should be ready by the time you're ready. And by the way, Grandma, I doubt you really need these lessons from Mark. You've been driving horses all your life. You probably know as much as he does."

Grandma Katie didn't respond. She just looked at Kaye, smiled and then turned around and headed for the bathroom.

Kaye wound the school day down and was able to count Wednesday as a productive day with her class. She had an art project at the end of the day making three-dimensional hearts that would be hung as mobiles from the light fixtures in the ceiling of her classroom. She had requested a ladder from the custodian to be able to do this, and the ladder had arrived a few minutes before school was dismissed. Cammy Jo had really enjoyed the project. Kaye never had any trouble keeping Cammy Jo's attention. The child was just an amazing bubble of delight in Kaye's day—a bubble that she didn't want to burst.

Mrs. Brown found Kaye on the ladder hanging hearts when she appeared in the doorway of the classroom. Kaye was expecting her but had her back to the doorway, and was startled when Mrs. Brown spoke. Several hearts fluttered to the floor and Kaye hugged the ladder when it rocked as she tried to catch the hearts floating away from her.

"I'm so sorry. I didn't mean to startle you," Mrs. Brown apologized. Kaye descended the ladder and had her feet firmly on the floor before responding, "I don't know why I was so startled, after all, I was expecting you."

Both ladies bent to the floor collecting paper hearts. The hearts were made from three different sources of paper: a red piece of construction paper, a white dolly, and another piece of pink construction paper that the children had been permitted to decorate any way they wished. Some had polka dots, some had stripes, and some of the boys had chosen to decorate theirs with souped-up cars. Kaye made no restrictions on what the students could use, so each heart was different and made a statement about each child.

Mrs. Brown studied each one as she picked them up. "These are very interesting, Miss Mason. You used individual creativity combining it with assemblage and sculpture techniques. Good for you and good for your students, too."

Kaye looked at Mrs. Brown trying to size the lady up. Here she was in what appeared to be the same outfit she had worn when she brought Cammy Jo to Kaye's class on the first day after Christmas break when school had resumed. Only today, in addition to the combat boots, she was wearing an oversized men's coat that was badly in need of a visit to the cleaners.

"You seem to know a lot about art, Mrs. Brown."

"That was my field of study when I attended college. I dropped out when I married my husband."

"Oh, I see," Kaye responded, knowing that she was really only seeing a little bit of what was happening in this woman's life.

After they had rescued the hearts from the floor, Kaye invited Mrs. Brown to sit down and was going to get her the only other adult chair in the room, which was situated in her reading group nook. "That's okay. You don't have to do that. I can just sit right here," Mrs. Brown said, taking a chair at a student's desk. The woman was so small that the child's chair was almost able to accommodate her comfortably. Kaye chose to sit on the child's desk next to Mrs. Brown for their talk.

"What did you need to see me about, Mrs. Brown?" Kaye asked trying not to stare at the way the lady was dressed.

"When Cammy Jo came home the day before school was cancelled for snow, she had Selby with her."

"Selby?" Kaye didn't quite understand.

"Yes. That's her stuffed toy. She slept with it for several years. Cammy Jo couldn't pronounce the 'h' in Shelby when she first got the toy. The name came out Selby and it just--sort of stuck."

"Oh, I see."

"Well, when I left my husband he allowed me to take clothes for the children but he wouldn't let me bring any of their toys along, so the only way I can figure that she could have gotten Selby, was for him to have brought it to her here."

"That's right, Mrs. Brown. He did bring the toy along with her backpack last Tuesday. Cammy Jo left both the backpack and the toy here Tuesday afternoon, but I guess she took the toy home with her on Wednesday before all that snow hit."

"Miss Mason, there was a lot of fighting between my husband and me, as well as an enormous amount of restrictions for me and for my kids when I was with my husband. Cammy Jo probably thought I'd be upset with her if she showed up where we live now with things her Dad brought to her."

"Maybe so, Mrs. Brown. I really can't say why Cammy Jo chose to leave those things at school."

"I know you can't keep him from coming here. I don't have a restraining order against him and I have no money to be able to get one. I just want you to know that I am trying hard to put my kids in a place where they can thrive. Yes, I had a beautiful house and lots of money with my husband, but it was a mental prison. Not only for me, but I felt it was for my children, too. My husband had to be in control of everything: bank accounts, what we ate. I went through rivers of tears trying to learn to cook everything just the way he wanted it. Don't get me wrong, I wanted for nothing materially. I even had beautiful clothes, but he picked out all of them. Just once in a while I would have liked to have selected something that I was going to wear."

Kaye continued to listen. She thought it important to let Mrs. Brown get it all out while she could. Besides, she didn't really know how to respond to the lady. There was an extended silence, however, and Kaye broke it by asking, "What happened to your beautiful clothes, Mrs. Brown?"

"Remember I said he let me take clothes for the children?"

"Yes."

"Well, in order to punish me, he wouldn't allow me to remove any of my clothes from the house. You'd have to live with him, Miss Mason, to realize what a control freak he is."

"Apparently," Kaye said, "but couldn't you get a court order to get your clothes, Mrs. Brown? Wouldn't the cabinet help you in some way?"

"The CPS protects children, Miss Mason. They only see me as an idiot for leaving that two-hundred thousand dollar house and moving in where I have."

"Mrs. Brown, I really shouldn't admit this, but Cammy Jo is a heart stealer. I didn't mean to, but I've become so attached to her in the short time I've had her in my classroom. So, please don't be upset with me when I ask you this, but I just have to know."

"What is it, Miss Mason? I'll try to tell you anything you need to know."

"Mrs. Brown, CPS has been here to talk with us about the children."

"I know. Cammy Jo told me the social worker had checked on her."

"Okay. I've never seen where you're living now, but the social worker was very concerned about a window being out in Cammy Jo's bedroom during the snow storm and when those temperatures dropped last week."

"The window has been covered in plastic. I have my own separate bedroom there and I took all my children in the room with me and we all slept together that night. They thought it was quite a fun thing to do. I would never let my kids be harmed, Miss Mason. I know I must look like a crazy loon moving from a nice subdivision to the place I live now, but my kids are free there. They can romp and play in the yard. At our other place, if they disturbed a blade of grass in the yard, they were yelled at. You should have seen the snowman they built last week! They would never have been allowed to do that under my husband's supervision. He wouldn't have allowed the snow to be trampled on or a silly thing like a snowman to be present in his yard. I'm looking forward to spring and summer when they can get outside, wade in the creek, catch fireflies and just be kids. Do you understand, Miss Mason?"

"I'm beginning to. Would you object, Mrs. Brown, to coming in to our Family Resource Center? It is staffed by two wonderful ladies. One is a registered social worker and she might be able to assist you with some of the legal issues. I know very little about law," Kaye admitted, thinking back to her former boyfriend, Chris, wondering how he would see and handle this situation. But she dismissed that idea knowing that this was the very thing a small-time lawyer might be caught up in, at a tiny town like Hope Springs where Chris's mother was vehemently opposed to him residing and having a law practice. She shook her head to clear her thoughts and then said, "Sorry, my mind drifted for a moment. The other things the FRC might be able to help you with is clothing. They run a clothes closet and they do have some clothes for adults as well as for children in it. You should give them a call."

"Thanks, Miss Mason. I might do that. I'd better go now. One of the boys is waiting for me in his car. It's the only means of transportation I have right now. You know if my husband wouldn't let me take my clothes with me, he sure wasn't going to let me have the car I used. Everything is in his name. So, I have no legal rights of ownership to anything, not the car or the house, and I suppose not even my clothes. I just thought you should know, Miss Mason, that leaving my husband took a lot of courage. I really didn't think I could do it, and I'll be forever indebted to the boys for opening their hearts and home to me and my children."

"I think you are wrong about what is justifiably yours, Mrs. Brown, but you would need an attorney's advice about that. Obviously, I did not pursue a legal degree."

With that Mrs. Brown stood, extended her hand to Kaye and said, "If there is anything Cammy Jo needs help with, let me know. She never brings home any homework, only books to read."

"She generally completes all her work in class, so she doesn't have a lot of homework. She's a pretty smart little gal, Mrs. Brown, and I don't assign much actual work that is required to be done at home."

"Okay, Miss Mason. Have a pleasant afternoon. I have taken up enough of your time. I'm sure you would like to get home some time today." Mrs. Brown smiled apologetically and was turning to leave the room when Kaye said, "Before you go, Mrs. Brown, there is one area where Cammy Jo could use some help. I noticed from her records that the other school did not have her enrolled in speech therapy. I have made a referral to the therapist for an informal evaluation to see if she would be a candidate."

"I hope you didn't mention that to her father when he was here. The other school did suggest that assistance. But you see, here is another area where everything had to be perfect in my husband's eyes. He said there was no need for speech therapy, that Cammy Jo was perfect the way she was, and that she would outgrow her language problems. Does he have to be present to give his approval for her to have the evaluation and the help?"

"I'm not sure, Mrs. Brown. I know that in the few special education meetings I have attended that only one parent was present at some of those meetings. The father usually did not attend due to having to take off from work to do so. In your case, I am not sure what to tell you. I guess things could get a little touchy. He might have to be notified, too. I'll check with our principal and he can check with the Special Education Supervisor at our central office. They may have to contact the school board attorney. Right now, I have no answer to your question as to whether Mr. Brown would have to be notified."

"Okay, after you get all that straightened out, let me know. I will be glad to sign for Cammy to get any help that she deserves. Have a good afternoon, Miss Mason," Mrs. Brown said and she turned and left the room.

Kaye was exhausted after teaching a full day and then listening to Mrs. Brown's story. She wasn't sure she had energy enough to climb back up that ladder and hang up those hearts. She made a trip to her desk first, found a sticky note and wrote: 'Mrs. Brown, FRC—clothes' and attached it to her lesson plan book. That way, she'd see it first thing on Thursday and alert them to Mrs. Brown's need for the clothing. Somehow she suspected they were already aware. Not much got past the attention of the office staff in that school.

As Kaye climbed the ladder to get all the hearts hung up, the references to 'the boys' that Mrs. Brown made, kept surfacing in Kaye's thoughts. *Just what are 'the boys' to her?* Kaye wondered.

She had just returned the ladder, placing it beside the custodian's door as she had been instructed to do, when Mrs. Adams came around the corner.

"Did the custodian tell you to leave that there?"

"Yes. He said he unlocks the building and comes in before anyone else each morning, and it would be put away before any students get here and have a chance to knock it over.

"I guess that would be okay, but let me get my master key and let's set it inside his office. So many groups use the school after hours and I know the basketball group will be here later. I wouldn't want any of them to get hurt or the ladder to disappear. We have a lot of things we need to spend money on for kids right now and a new ladder isn't one of them. How do you think your kids will do on the spring tests, Kaye?"

"I hope they'll be fine, but since I've never administered one of those tests. I can't really say for sure."

"Yes, well, it's a relief to have the testing over when school is finished in May, but then you have to wait all summer until next fall for the results. By the way, how did the conference with Mrs. Brown go?"

"Let's go get your key and then go sit down somewhere. I have quite a lot to tell you about the things I heard during that conference today. I wish you could have been there. You might have been more help to her than I was. I was just stumped and didn't know what to say about all the things she told me."

Chapter 13

The remaining days of the month of February did not bring any additional snow or dangerously freezing temperatures to the state of Kentucky. Kaye worked hard on lesson plans. She conferred with her teaching team in an attempt to find the most interesting things that she could do that would meet the demands of the spring testing requirements, while at the same time, hoping that she was adding a desire for learning to the class. She found this was a most difficult task. Kaye lamented to her grandmother over breakfast one morning that she feared that state requirements were taking a lot of the fun and joy away from teaching, and more importantly, taking the fun and joy away from the task of learning for her students.

"You know, Grandma, when I was in second grade, I had a teacher who did a unit on Japan. I don't know why she did it. None of the other teachers did, but they didn't work together to plan as much back then. I know they didn't because of the complaints I hear now about the requirements for cooperative planning sessions from some of the more experienced teachers. I don't think teaching about Japan was even on the curriculum plan at second grade level, or if there even was a curriculum plan back then, but she made that unit so interesting that I still remember the things we did."

"What did she do that makes it stand out in your mind so much, Kaye?"

"She had a lady come to the classroom to speak who had been to Japan. She wore a kimono and brought in some of her doll collection."

"I bet that was eye catching."

"It was! Then she sent recipes home to parents. They cooked the dishes and brought them to school and ate with us. I guess she either bought a box of chopsticks or had them donated by an oriental restaurant and we all got to try eating with them. Then we got to take the chopsticks home. We thought we had a grand treasure."

"You're kidding. Second graders and chopsticks! I hope she had some back-up plastic spoons and forks."

"Oh, she did, Grandma. But I think she got in a little trouble when a couple of the boys got the chopsticks out on the bus on the way home and had a chopstick sword fight." Katie laughed and Kaye continued talking about her teacher. "She had someone come to the class who knew about origami. They demonstrated and fascinated us with the things they made and then we got to make an origami bird. I remember Mom put a string and a hook on mine and hung it in the kitchen window."

"Well, maybe teachers had more freedom in planning what they would do with their students back then. I hope you find some answers to your planning dilemma that will make you feel better about this. But speaking of your mother, they will be here this weekend for your three-day mini-vacation. You did say that you would be off for Presidents' Day, didn't you? We need to finalize plans for your wedding. Are you ready for that, Kaye?"

"I think so. Seems like all I do is plan these days, Grandma. Plan lessons, plan for a wedding. It never stops."

"Kaye, my dear, God gives us every day that we live and breathe. So I feel that each day deserves a well thought-out plan, one that deserves the efforts put into doing it."

Jean and Bill left Paducah early on Friday afternoon so they could meet the family in Hope Springs and enjoy eating a meal out rather than Katie having to spend time cooking dinner. Besides, the dining room table was once again loaded with wedding paraphernalia.

Tom arrived at the diner a little before Kaye and her family did and was surprised to see Julie and Jerry Mayhugh there with their children. He studied Jerry as he alternated taking bites of his meal while spooning mashed potatoes into his daughter's mouth. The little one patted the tray on the high chair and kicked her feet while smiling at her daddy. Then she picked up a roll, stuffing a fair amount of it in her mouth before attempting to bite into it. "Wook, Mommy, Mandy willy yikes her woll."

"Yes, Andrew. She's being really good. So are you. Your are learning to use that fork so well."

"Yeah, deez mashed potatoes are berry good."

The bell over the diner door jangled and all heads turned as Kaye and her family entered. Roth immediately approached Julie and Jerry's table shaking Jerry's hand. Then pulled back and reached for a napkin. He realized that part of Mandy's meal was attached to Jerry's hand and he now had the residue of Mandy's dinner on his hand, too.

"Oh, sorry, Roth," Jerry apologized and handed Roth another napkin. "Hazards of the trade of fatherhood."

Roth wiped his hand on the napkin, smiled, and said, "No problem."

Julie smiled and said, "I don't know, sometimes, who wears the most of Mandy's meals, Jerry or Mandy."

"When do we get to have another jam session, Jerry?" Roth wanted to know.

"Kaye asked me about that the last time we saw her, and we just haven't gotten around to it. It's hard to get away from the kids," Jerry laughed patting Mandy on the head.

"Why would you want to get away from this little cutie?" Jean asked holding out her hands to Mandy. Mandy smiled and reached for Jean.

"Are you watching this, Tom? You're going to have to get busy and give this family some of these," Jerry joked, pointing to his children.

"Do you mind if I wait until after this wedding these ladies are planning, Jerry? You're proposing something that could get me in a lot of trouble," Tom replied while loosening the collar of his shirt.

"I think that might be advisable, Tom. If you get Kaye pregnant now, the wedding dress probably won't fit," Julie added.

Trying to change the subject, Tom asked, "By the way, Julie, how did the painting you selected work out?"

"It's great! You should come see where I put it. In fact, why don't we do the next jam session at our house? That way we wouldn't need a baby sitter. As much as I'd like to get away for a while, sitters are expensive and you can't always find a reliable one. How about tomorrow night? Bill and Jean, will you still be here?"

"Yes, we are in for the weekend," Jean replied. "I don't play a thing. Can't carry a tune in a bucket, but if I can play with Mandy and this handsome young man, I'll come."

Introducing himself, Andrew said, "My name is Androo, but my pairwents call me Andy."

"I'm very pleased to meet you, Andy. Is it alright if I call you Andy, too?" Jean asked.

"It's all wight," Andy replied.

"How about it folks? Want to go to Jerry and Julie's tomorrow night?" Jean asked. Everyone chimed in, "Yes," with a lot of head nodding.

"I'll bring a dessert," Katie added.

"I'll pitch in soft drinks," Tom offered, "and will bring extra ice."

"We'll stop and get some munchies," Jean pitched in.

"Are you going to leave anything for me to do?" Julie asked.

"Nope," Kaye added, "I'll get paper plates and we're good. You folks just get ready to play while you have Mom to entertain the kids. I bet Dad will even help out in that area."

"You bet," Bill affirmed.

Jean looked at Mandy and Andy thinking: *Maybe selling the house and the business and moving here wouldn't be such a bad thing. If we do get grandkids, I really don't want to be hours away.*

Then she said, "We will be looking forward to tomorrow night with a lot of pleasure. I can't wait."

After a great night at the diner, Kaye and her family spent the next morning with wedding plans. Invitations were selected. Napkins were ordered.

Jean had a surprise for everyone when a caterer showed up around 1:00 p.m. She and Bill had decided that the wedding day should not be an event that exhausted everyone by having to prepare food and haul it to a reception hall.

Kaye selected a menu, but called Tom to confer with him to make sure everything would suit him, too. All Tom could think, without saying it out loud was: *Hell, Kaye, I'll probably be too nervous to eat anyway and you'll be too busy. Just get something most folks would like.* But instead he said, "Sounds fine to me. Have you decided on a cake, yet?"

"No, that's next. She has over one hundred pictures of cakes. I don't know which one I want."

"Can I put in a request?" Tom asked.

"Of course you can. What is it?"

"Make one layer be a hummingbird cake. Probably needs to be the bottom layer. It's a real heavy cake. My Aunt used to make them for our holiday get-togethers and family reunions. It's a wonder I didn't get sick. Don't know why a cake that would cause you to gain five pounds would be named after a little bird that doesn't weigh hardly anything. I'd eat so much of that cake that afterwards, I would have to pray for forgiveness for committing gluttony."

"It's done, Tom. I'll make sure one layer is hummingbird. By the way, are you nearly ready to come over? We have an appointment in town at the tuxedo rentals at 3:30. Mom and I have decided to take a weekend trip later and look at wedding gowns in a larger city. We'll grab an early supper and then head over to Jerry and Julie's, if that's okay."

"Sounds like you have it all planned," Tom replied, thinking: *Wonder if the rest of my life will be this well planned out for me. Probably will. I'm marrying a teacher.*

Picking out the tuxedo proved to be a quick and easy task. So Kaye phoned her family and they all met outside town at the restaurant where Mark had taken Kaye to eat last summer. The young couple that had purchased and renovated it had made great strides since Kaye was last there. The bed and breakfast was going well and they were planning on adding a much larger dining hall. They hoped the room would be rented out for banquets, family reunions, marriage receptions, graduation parties, and other celebrations. The young couple was just brimming with ideas. They had finally named the place and hung a sign out front that read: Tollhouse Restaurant, Bed and Breakfast.

Bill looked at the rest of the party and said, "If they have that room ready by the time of the wedding, maybe you could have your reception here."

"We'll think about that Dad," Kaye said looking questioningly at Tom.

"Tollhouse Restaurant," Katie said, "reminds me of a chocolate chip cookie."

"Sure does," Jean added, "and it's turning into a real sweet place. Maybe it would be a good place for the reception. Tom, what do you think?"

Tom's reply was, "I think we need to let them get the room added on to their place, take a look at it then, and see if it meets with everyone's fancy."

"Good thinking, guy," Roth confirmed. "Now, let's get on out to Julie and Jerry's place. I want to hear some good music and I'd kind of like to see that little Mandy again."

"Even if she's all smeared with the remnants of her dinner?" Katie asked with a little smirk of a smile.

"Here," Roth said, handing Katie the extra napkins from their dinner table. "Better take these along, just in case I get mashed potato fingers again."

Chapter 14

The weekend ended too soon with the family going their separate ways. Jean and Bill would be headed back to Paducah. But before they left, Kaye confirmed the first weekend in April to be the date to pick out the wedding dress. She and Jean decided to make it a mother–daughter weekend. Katie bowed out when she heard the plans, thinking it would be too much for her. Kaye would drive home to Paducah on Friday after she got out of school. They could look in some shops in Paducah Saturday morning, drive to Louisville, look there in the afternoon, spend the night and then drive to Lexington and look some more.

"My gosh, girls, why don't you just get an airline ticket and check out what New York has to offer?" Bill kidded them.

"We could, Dad. The next week is spring break," Kaye kidded right back. "We don't have to be in a hurry."

"Oh, no! I have a feeling this is really going to cost me," Bill said with a very worried frown wrinkling his forehead.

"Don't worry, Dad. We'll find the perfect dress."

"That's what I am afraid of. It may not exactly have the perfect price, but you certainly should have enough choices, with all the places you two are going."

Kaye had just smiled and kissed her Dad on top of the head while she handed him a second cup of coffee before he and Jean left to go back to Paducah that morning. Whoa! Did she see a small bald spot forming? That thought entered her head several times that day and she knew that when she returned from finding that wedding gown that she was going to spend some time in Paducah with her Dad, too, since Mom would have her for the weekend. Watching the people who mattered most to her ageing was a scary thing. She only knew she wanted to make sure the time they had left was well spent. She would take Grandma Katie's advice and plan every day with a well thought-out plan that deserved the efforts being put into it.

Tom was busy getting fertilizer on all the fields before the weather broke and the ground became too soft. He didn't need his tractors marring down in the slop of spring-thawed muddy earth that often happened in Kentucky.

While in Hope Springs getting a buggy full of fertilizer hooked up to his truck, an Amish father and son came into the feed and seed store. Tom didn't want to live an Amish lifestyle, but he had always admired what appeared to be their very orderly, calm way of living. He had been to several of their spring auctions, which they called mud sales. Very muddy fields often were the result as people pulled their horse drawn and motorized vehicles into the fields to attend the sales. It was seldom that the Amish had a true parking lot available. A few commercial buildings had gravel access and driveways. Tom realized that "the English," as the Amish called the people in America who were not Amish, needed a place to park automobiles. The Amish, however, were parking horse drawn buggies and they didn't need paved parking lots.

Tom knew that the Amish people had their own set of problems, but the manners displayed by their young children seemed almost unnaturally obedient. He knew the young boys shadowed their fathers and wondered if some day he'd have a shadow. He liked that thought. He smiled and tipped his hat to the young boy standing by his father. The child looked at Tom, smiled, but didn't move and remained silent under his small straw hat.

Roth waved goodbye to Katie, and settled down in the kitchen for a second cup of coffee. Mark had called last evening and asked if Katie could come a day early for her driving lesson, that he needed to drive to Versailles the next day to look at another horse that someone wanted him to train.

The phone rang just as Roth got his coffee fixed the way he wanted it. When he answered, he heard Mark at the other end.

"Hey, Roth, what are you up to tomorrow? It just occurred to me that I don't have to go to Versailles alone. Why don't you ride up with me and take a look at this horse. I really wouldn't mind having your opinion. He's supposed to be quite a handful and I'm not so sure I should take this one on."

Roth hesitated a moment and then smiled and agreed to go. "I think I'd enjoy that, Mark. It might be nice to get away from all this cake and lace and wedding planning for a day."

"Okay, ol' buddy, you're on. I'll pick you up around nine. Will that be okay?"

"Sure will," Roth answered. "See you then."

Yeah, by nine I should be finished with another one of those oatmeal breakfasts Katie insists I eat since I had that by-pass surgery. Cholesterol! What other life restrictions will doctors come up with next? Roth was beginning to long for the days of bacon and egg breakfasts with a nice biscuit and some sausage gravy thrown over it. *Oh, well,* he thought, *should be thankful I'm alive and able to go look at a horse.* He settled back in his chair and flipped his paper open to read.

When Katie arrived at the barn, she found Mark in his office busy at his computer. "Oh, Miss Katie! Come here and see what you think about this."

Katie looked over his shoulder at what appeared to be a brochure. "What do you think? One of the kids who works and rides here designed it for me."

"It looks nice. It's amazing what young folks can do with computers these days. What's it for, Mark?"

"Two things actually. One is to advertise my stable and the lessons and training I offer. The other is to advertise a camp I will offer during spring break. The schools are having some career days and have asked me to come and speak. I thought if I could have these to hand out to the kids, they could take them home and parents would get to see what I offer."

"Looks good and sounds good to me," Katie replied as Mark printed a copy and handed it to her.

"Miz Katie, after you drive Secret today, I'd like you to drive one of my lesson horses. Then think about this: How would you like to help out at my spring break camp? You could teach some of the older students to drive."

"Oh, Mark! My goodness! Are you sure I could do that? I've never taught anybody anything other than a Sunday school lesson."

"I'm more than positive that's not so, Miss Katie. You have no idea how much you teach people. Just think about it and discuss it with Roth, who, by the way, I just spoke to on the phone while you were on your way over here, and he's going to ride along with me to Versailles tomorrow and look at a horse someone wants me to train."

"Oh, that's great, Mark. He really needs to get out of the house. This winter weather is a little hard on him anymore and I think he's got a good case of cabin fever right now. Going with you will do him good."

"Speaking of going, Miguel has Secret ready. So, we better get going with your training."

Kaye was back at work and successfully ending her day when the principal showed up at her door with Officer Howell. Since he was the DARE Officer assigned to Hope Springs Elementary,

Kaye was not surprised to see him but felt a little odd at both men's presence in her room after school.

"I'm sorry to do this to you, Kaye. I wouldn't let the officer come until school was out. Didn't want you to be upset. I know teachers do not like to be served with summons."

"Summons?!" Kaye exclaimed, "For what? What have I done?"

"You haven't done anything, Miss Mason. You just need to appear for a deposition for a custody case," the officer explained.

Kaye stood there in silence until the officer held out the papers to her. "I suppose I have to take these whether I want to or not. I really don't appreciate being drawn into people's court cases regarding their children," Kaye said as she took the envelope.

"None of us do, Kaye," the principal replied, "but several of us received these today and I didn't want you to get yours and be upset in front of your students."

"I appreciate that," Kaye replied, opening the envelope and unfolding the papers. "Oh, it's regarding the Brown children. What on earth do they want from me?"

"None of us are sure, Kaye, but CHR will be here tomorrow to enlighten us. There's apparently a lot going on."

"Okay. Thank you, Officer Howell, I *think*."

"No thanks needed, Kaye. Sorry about this. It's just part of my job."

The two men left the room and Kaye sat down to look more closely at the summons. It was then that she saw the names of the attorneys representing the Brown parents. An attorney from the county attorney's office was representing Mrs. Brown. Kaye supposed the lady had been assigned a public defender. But Chris Wilshire, Attorney at Law, was representing Mr. Brown.

Well, I guess he passed his bar exams. Will he never get out of my life? Kaye thought. *Guess not, at least not right now.* She could just see herself giving a deposition to Chris Wilshire. *Guess he's involved in small town divorce cases after all. His mother wouldn't like that, now would she?* Kaye thought and smiled with some satisfaction. Then the smile disappeared. There was something really fishy about this. Why would Chris be handling this case?

The horse trailer bounced and rattled as Mark pulled into the barn lot at Crawford's Saddlebred Farm. John Parker, the trainer at the farm, met them at the truck and ushered them into the barn. "The horse will be ready in a few minutes, Mark. He wants to go the minute we get him tacked up, so I didn't want him standing too long in harness. We'll lunge him first. If you want, I'll ride him after we saddle him. That way you can see what he's like from the ground before you get in the irons."

"May not want to get in the irons if he's as ornery as you say, but it sounds like a plan. Let's go."

Roth watched with admiration as John worked the horse. The horse was a descendent of Coal Train, a glistening black beauty of a horse. His leg action was superb, conformation was excellent and he loved to play. This was evident when John reversed the horse in the lines and the horse turned with several bucks before settling down. When John brought him to a halt, the horse reared, standing on his hind legs for several seconds, pawing the air. Then he stood surprisingly still while John collected the lunge lines and held him for the groom to remove the harness and place a saddle on him.

John worked the horse through all five gaits. The 'rack' and 'rack on' were marvelous. The horse had a true slow gait and an amazingly fast, full-out racking gait. He balked at the canter, however, and it took several tries before he decided he would accept John's signal. His canter did seem smooth, however, once he decided to do it.

"Mark, he has all the action of a champion in that trot. You can't get legs up much higher than that. What are you going to do ol' chum?" Roth asked after observing the horse.

"I'll ride him, see if he handles as well for me as for John, and then decide. I've got my trailer. I can take him home today."

Mark mounted the horse and found he had the same trouble with the horse as John. He was reluctant to take his canter lead. *Wonder what brought this about?* Mark thought, trying to consider what things could have gone wrong in this horse's training.

When he dismounted, Roth asked, "Well, Mark, what's the verdict? Think you can straighten out that canter?"

"Don't know, but never will if I don't give it a try, will I? What say we load him up and give him a month with me and then see what we've got."

"I think it's well worth the try. That horse is Louisville material if I ever saw one. What's his name?"

"Don't know."

"You don't know much of anything today, do you, son?" Roth teased.

"Guess not," Mark replied and then suggested, "Let's get some paperwork and find out."

John gave Mark and Roth all the paperwork necessary to haul the horse back to Mark's barn. They watched as John loaded a very calm horse named Midnight's Sensation in Mark's trailer.

"Well, we know he loads without any trouble. At least we know that much," Roth laughed and smacked Mark on the back after Mark closed the trailer door.

On a handshake with John, Midnight's trainer, and Mr. Crawford, John's dad and Midnight's owner, Mark agreed to keep the horse in training at his barn for one month. A very happy Roth and an excited Mark drove back to Hope Springs. Mark's thoughts were, *I may have a five-gaited contender for the World Championship in Louisville this year.*

Tom answered the door to a very apologetic Richard Mallory. "I'm very sorry it has taken me so long to come and get these paintings. If many more things had come up, Marty would have been back home and could have come for them herself."

"That's okay. They're not in the way yet. But my fiancé will want them gone before she moves in in June, I'm sure."

"Probably so. How did you come to have them here, Mr. Scott?"

"Call me Tom, please. Only my Little League guys call me Mr. Scott, and that's only because their parents insist."

"Fair enough, and please call me Richard. But I would still like to know how these painting came to be at your house."

"Come on and I'll show them to you," Tom pointed to the stairway and Mr. Mallory followed listening to Tom's story. "Marty and I were good friends. She used to come out sometimes and spend the weekend and paint."

"Oh, I see," Richard responded, silently adding *I bet that's not all she spent her weekend doing.*

"When she decided to accept the grant to study in France," Tom continued, "she had nowhere to store her paintings, so I offered my vacant bedroom upstairs."

Tom opened the door letting Richard go through first. He was amazed at the number of canvases stacked around the walls of the room. "I heard you say you're engaged, Tom. I can imagine your prospective wife has ideas for the room that do not include storing another woman's artwork."

"She wouldn't mind keeping some of it--or at least she's teased me about putting one of the pictures of a male that is very nude in her bathroom." Richard stopped leafing through the paintings long enough to enjoy a good laugh.

"I haven't come across that one yet, Tom. Do you want to keep it?" Richard asked with a big hint of merriment in his eyes and a twisted little smile.

"No, thanks, Richard. I kind of vetoed that idea. I'm no judge of art, but I wonder if some of those are even Marty's work. You know what I mean? Some are so different."

"Well, you know artists, Tom." Tom couldn't say that he really did. The only artist he had known was Marty. "They go through different periods of expression," Richard explained.

"I guess," Tom replied.

"I'll look for signatures later when I get them back to my place. I'll be under better light there and will be better able to authenticate the artist."

"Won't Marty be home soon? Wouldn't she be able to do that for you?"

"I spoke to Marty yesterday and it seems like she may have a number of options open to her about coming home."

"Like what?" Tom wanted to know.

"She has been noticed for her work in Europe as well as here. By the way, I do want to take all of these. They may bring a very high price someday. I have plenty of storage space, so it's not a problem for me."

I bet you do, Tom thought. Then he was hearing Kaye's concerns about how much Marty might or might not profit from Mallory being an agent for her paintings. "Do you really think Marty might become well-known enough to make a living painting?"

"Can't ever say for sure, Tom. Right now it's purely speculation, but she's good enough that I'm willing to invest the time to take the risk."

"Well, tell her we'd all like to see her back here in Hope Springs."

"I'll do that but she may not be back in the states for a while. She has a chance to go to Belgium and Sweden to do some study in Dutch painting. She'd be a visiting professor in Belgium for a few months before going to Sweden. She also has some offers from some school systems and a university in New York City. I don't think she knows what she wants to do right now."

This sure is a come-up from being a waitress at a diner, Tom thought. "Well, whatever she decides, I hope it turns out to be the best choice for her," Tom added.

"Me, too," Richard agreed. "Now, how about we start carrying paintings out to my van? I sure am glad you are here to assist. When I get back to NYC, I'll have my crew to help me."

Richard shook Tom's hand when the last painting was securely placed in the van and his parting words were, "Now you and your fiancé can turn that room into a nursery if you need to."

Tom smiled, shook Richard's hand and said, "Thanks, Richard, and be careful with Marty's paintings. Drive safe."

"I will," Richard assured Tom. *I'll be more careful than ever now. I might even have some nursery plans of my own now that I know for sure that Tom Scott is out of any plans Marty might have had,* Richard thought. *Oh, well, who can tell what Marty will do next? She's an artist.* Richard continued talking to himself. *It's just that I am not usually as attracted to my clients as I am to her. But it could work. She creates, I promote. Speaking of promotions, I need to check my map and reprogram the GPS in my phone. Those folks in Alabama want to know what I can do for them, too. Hope the actual work is as good as their pictures,* and Richard continued on down the road with Marty on his mind.

Chapter 15

"Kaye, we already have a call from Mr. Brown this morning. Here's his number. He wants you to call him." Abby, the attendance clerk had taken the call from Mr. Brown earlier that morning and was delivering the phone message to Kaye. Kaye reached for the contact information saying, "Wonder what he wants now?"

"No telling, Kaye. Wouldn't it be nice if we could just teach these kids? I have to take time today to do an attendance report that has to be presented at a deposition hearing."

"My gosh! Have they subpoenaed the whole school staff?!" Kaye exclaimed.

"Almost," Abby replied.

The morning routine of teaching went well and Kaye called Mr. Brown during her planning period. He told her he was attempting to be appointed primary custodial parent for his children. He said he could not stand to think about his children being in the living conditions where his wife had placed them. Kaye listened and Mr. Brown added that he had been offered a position in Lexington that would mean a significant raise in pay for him. He stated that it would almost double what he was earning now. He was more than certain that he could provide for all his family's needs with no problem. He could even afford to hire a nanny if needed.

Kaye hung up the phone wondering what would be best for the Brown kids, living with their mother or with their father.

Then she realized that what she thought wouldn't matter one little bit. It would be what the judge thought that mattered most.

She wondered if Mrs. Brown would appear in front of the judge in the combat boots and articles of clothing she had come to the school wearing. On one side, the lady would look demented. On the other side, she would appear abused if the judge knew why she was dressed like she was. Would the judge find out that Mr. Brown was punishing his wife by not letting her have her clothes? The lady was indeed in a mess, one that might cause her to lose her children.

Kaye remembered that Mr. Brown had said, "Miss Mason, I really do not want to divorce my wife. I'd take her back in a minute if she'd just come to her senses." The problem was Kaye couldn't tell who the crazy person was: the overly restrictive father or the 'let's all be free' mother. Maybe they both were crazy. Wouldn't she just love to wave a magic wand and make Cammy Jo her own?

It was time to go get her students from their library time. She looked at the books they had selected to read during the coming week as they exited the library. Cammy Jo was at the back of the line and was the last to show Kaye her book. Cammy Jo took Kaye's hand with a big smile and they walked back to the classroom. Kaye was at the verge of considering kidnapping this kid. *What a ridiculous thought,* she admitted to herself, *but it eases my mind a little to give it consideration, even if it is not at all possible.*

The people from Child Protective Services met with the student team after school to explain what would be expected from them. It seemed to Kaye that the objective of the CPS workers was to get the children out of the place where they were living. Kaye listened and tried to conceive how anything the school personnel could possibly do or say would strengthen the case to remove the children from their mother. She supposed they'd be placed with their father since he had the means to support them and the room to house them. She knew those were usually the requirements that qualified people to take possession of children.

Mr. Brown seemed so poised and capable. He also appeared to be very hurt by not having his children with him. Kaye knew, however, that material wealth certainly helped in raising children, but it absolutely didn't promise happiness in anyone's life. Some of her poorest children were the happiest. What really plagued her was Cammy Jo's reluctance to be with her father the day he brought her backpack and stuffed animal to school. She had never appeared unhappy at any other time. But that day was not one that was happy for her. Cammy Jo had worn a look of concern for the rest of that day.

Kaye knew the attendance clerk would report perfect attendance. Cammy Jo hadn't missed a day of school. Kaye would report having a very bright and happy little student. What would the judge think? What would he or she decide? She was glad she wasn't the one having to make the decision.

Kaye went into the main office to collect her mail after the meeting with CPS. The driver from Cammy Jo's bus, having finished her afternoon bus route, came into the office waving a summons paper saying, "Anyone know what this is about? I've been summoned to give a deposition about the Brown children! What can I possibly tell them? Cute, happy little girl lives with her brother and mother in a hell hole?"

Oh, my gosh! Kaye thought. *That bus driver might have testimony that would become the deciding factor. She delivers Cammy Jo to that home everyday. She actually sees the conditions—at least from the outside.* Then it occurred to her: *Chris has left no stone unturned. Boy! He has really done his homework on this one. Wonder if he is somehow connected to the firm in Lexington that has offered Mr. Brown the new job?*

Kaye walked the hallway back to her room feeling like her heart might stop beating. She closed her door and hit the floor on her knees. The tears started flowing and her prayer was: *Please, Lord, look down here and help me. Please let whatever comes out of my mouth be to Cammy Jo's benefit. Please help us to help her. And, Lord, I guess I should say a prayer for the parents, too. I won't even say let them solve their differences and get back together and take care of their children. I know both of them want to take care of their kids. I will just say let your will be done and please, please, watch over Tom and me in the future. May we always receive grace from you so that we look out and take care of each other. I know if we do that first, it will make it that much easier to care for any children that we might be blessed to have.*

Kaye ended her prayer and then began talking to herself. *Okay, Kaye, get up off your knees. It's Tuesday, line dance night with Tom, and you still have a ton of papers to grade.* She started stuffing a canvas bag with her grade book and the papers she needed to take with her. She wiped her eyes once more and headed out the door, arms full.

Kaye skipped supper that night with her grandparents. Grandma Katie knew something was wrong, but heeding Roth's earlier advice, kept quiet waiting for Kaye to talk to her. She was a bit disappointed when Kaye, dressed in her jeans and dancing boots, disappeared out the door with Tom.

On the way to the Silver Saddle, Tom said, "Okay, out with it. What's bothering you?"

"I don't know if I like the way you can read me, Tom. I'll never be able to hide anything from you."

"Don't want you hiding things from me. Now what's wrong?"

Kaye proceeded to tell him about the subpoena to give a deposition, the call from Mr. Brown, and the visit from Child Protective Services.

"Brace yourself, Kaye. Might as well get ready for a visit from Mrs. Brown. That will be next."

"Tom, there's more and it really has me concerned. When I looked closely at the summons, the attorney listed for Mr. Brown was Chris Wilshire."

"Tell me you're joking."

"I wish I were."

"Thought he was working for some big firm in Lexington. What's he doing handling a custody case in Hope Springs?"

"I don't know unless the job being offered to Mr. Brown is somehow affiliated with the law firm where Chris is working."

"Wonder if he knows you are Cammy Jo's teacher?"

"I'd think he'd have to know. I mean, he had to sign the request for the deposition so he had to see my name."

"Well, this will be interesting."

"I wish interesting was all. Suppose I say something that hurts Cammy Jo or turns out not to be in her best interest? I couldn't stand that."

"Oh, Kaye, you couldn't hurt that kid. What could happen to cause that?"

"I don't know. I just have an awful feeling about it. But let's concentrate on us for a while. I need to dance. More, I need to dance and be held by you."

"I can arrange that," Tom said as he pulled into a parking space at the Silver Saddle and shut the engine down.

Chapter 16

Chris Wilshire, Attorney at Law. Things seemed to be rolling along quite well since Chris had joined the firm and he liked seeing that title following his name. He wondered why, though, the firm had assigned him to a custody case. This wasn't the kind of thing his firm usually handled. The buzz around the office was that one of the partners had a stepbrother who needed some help. Still why not refer this stepbrother to a good divorce attorney?

Chris could ask a lot of questions, but since he was new to the firm, he thought he'd better not rock the boat. Still, if this was a partner's stepbrother, he better not lose the case either. He was beginning to feel the pressure when he opened the file and started leafing through the papers in it.

He stopped when he saw the child named Cammy was enrolled in Hope Springs Elementary. Then he looked closely at the summons and drew in a sharp breath when he realized Kaye Mason was the child's teacher. How had he missed seeing that when the legal assistant had him to signed the papers so the summons for depositions could be filed and served? He had to find a way to dismiss himself from being Mr. Brown's attorney. Could he possibly be seen as a risk to the case since he and Kaye had not parted on good terms?

How would she feel about being questioned by him? Could he send someone else and just advise? This was truly going to be a sticky situation. He felt like he was already stuck. Might as well be super glued to his chair. He couldn't seem to be able to even think about how to get up and start to get unglued from this mess.

Chris left work late and went to the apartment he had rented since moving out of his parent's home. The phone rang. It was Arnold Samuels inviting him out for a drink.

"I think I'll pass, Arnold."

"What's wrong, buddy? You don't sound too good."

"Just tired, I guess. But, Arnold, before you go, do you know anything about a partner with a stepbrother who is suing to be the custodial parent of his three kids?"

"Can't say that I do, buddy, but I can ask around. Do a little investigating if you'd like. You know there are a few people around there that know everything about everybody."

Chris actually didn't know that. He'd been much too busy to take part in inner office gossip.

"Tell you what, let me see what I can find out. What's the stepbrother's name?"

"Brown."

"We don't have any attorneys named Brown."

"I know that."

"Must have different fathers."

"Guess so."

"Let me do a little witch hunting. But why is this so important to you?"

"I have been assigned to the case."

"You're shitting me! Why would they assign you? There's a ton of good divorce attorneys in this city."

"I don't know, Arnold. I don't even know if the guy wants a divorce. He is only, at the moment, trying to become the primary custodial parent. Seems the kids are living in some really poor conditions and he wants them out of there."

"You met Brown, then?"

"Talked to him on the phone. Did some preliminary work, depositions and such."

"Are you pissed off about this, Chris? I know it's not the kind of cases you've been doing. Do you think they're dumping on you?"

"No, Arnold. There's something else that has me concerned. Let's talk about it tomorrow. In the meantime, be careful with your snooping and try not to get me or you in trouble."

"Will do my best, Chris. See you in the morning."

Roth had Katie all to himself. It was Tuesday night and Kaye was line dancing with Tom. He liked having his granddaughter with them, but the time alone with Katie was something he prized, too.

Lately, Katie seemed more energetic and bright eyed than ever. He could only surmise that driving the horse over at Mark's place had brought about the change.

He found her standing in the door of the laundry room. "Penny for your thoughts."

Katie turned around laughing and replied, "My thoughts would cost you a lot more than a penny."

"Really," Roth replied, "Tell me."

"Oh, Roth, it's just a silly wishing idea."

"Tell me and I'll tell you if I feel like it's silly."

"I was just thinking about what I'd like to do to this room."

"Well, you've folded enough laundry in it that I'm afraid you're going to tell me you'd like to blow it to hell."

"Really, Roth, you can be so ridiculous sometimes."

"Okay, tell me what you want to do." Roth stood with his mouth open while Katie described the changes she was envisioning.

"I'd open the room up with more light. Extend it a bit and put in a door back there on the back wall. Put shelves and cabinets along this wall. Add some outlets—one just outside the door where I'd put a small patio with a work table so I could keep the mess of cleaning gourds outside."

Roth swallowed, thought a few seconds and confirmed, "You want a craft room in other words."

"Yes, I could still do laundry in here, but could set my sewing machine up, leave it, and still have room to cut out patterns. There would also be plenty of room to store my gourd supplies."

"Why, if you had all that to take up your time, I'd never get a meal fixed. You'd spend all your time in here. Between this and driving horses, I'd never see you."

"Don't be silly, Roth. But speaking of driving horses. Mark is going to have a youth camp at his barn during spring break and wants me to give driving lessons. The kids would attend lectures, ride and drive and I think he's even planning a trail ride with a chuck wagon cookout."

"He wants you to teach kids how to drive?"

"That's what he said."

"Are you going to do it?"

"I'm thinking about it. Would you mind?"

"I think you'd enjoy that, Katie. Just don't get hurt."

The phone rang and Roth went back into the kitchen to answer. It was Mark. "Why, hello, Mark! Heard you offered my wife a job."

"Sure did, Roth. I've got so many horses to train and people to train riding them that I'm going to have to hire extra help."

"Glad business is so good for you, Mark. That's great!"

"I think so. Has Katie decided to give the camp during spring break a try?"

"I think she has."

"Well, that's good. I'm glad to hear that because I want to run something else by her."

"What's that, Mark?"

"A group of mothers came by to see me this morning. Some are mothers of kids who ride here, some aren't. They put a proposal before me that could be quite profitable. They want a mother's morning at the barn. Just them, no kids. They want to learn to ride and drive. If Katie and I took them on, we could use Miguel, too, and rotate them between riding lessons with me, driving lesson with her, and horse care—you know, grooming, saddling, and all the stuff with Miguel. What do you think? How do you feel about Katie putting in an extra morning at the barn with me? Or, to tell you the truth, Roth, she could come and drive Secret on Thursday afternoon when Kaye comes for her lesson. Then she could use the morning time she spends driving Secret now, to train the Morning Moms. Katie just needs to work with the horse. She really doesn't need my instruction. You know that, I'm sure."

"I think you better talk to Katie, Mark. It's really up to her to decide."

When Katie hung up the phone, she looked at Roth and asked, "What do you think?" She had never worked outside the home before and she wasn't quite sure how Roth really felt about all this.

He responded by saying, "Well, Katie, my girl, if you really want to remodel that laundry room you better get to work and earn some money." Then he laughed and said, "You've paid the bills long enough around here that you know there's plenty of money to redo that room. If you want to teach at Mark's barn, I suggest you do it. I personally think you'll have a ball."

Katie just smiled and hugged her husband. When Roth let her go he watched her walk away, loving the sight of his wife. He'd admired her backside for so many years and he never got tired of seeing it. He knew, however, that he had double reasons for wanting Katie to teach those lessons. She had devoted herself to and built her life around him and the farm, and he often wondered how she'd fill up the hours of her day without him around. He always figured he'd precede her in death and he knew she was smart enough to keep busy and teaching at Mark's barn would be a great investment of her time. Plus, he'd get busy on that craft room. That ought to give her plenty to do in her spare time.

When Kaye got home from line dance lessons she was elated to hear the news. Plus, if Grandma Katie drove Secret on

Thursday nights when she had her riding lesson, she'd get to spend more time with her.

Mark spent a whole day at the middle school with classes rotating in and out of his lecture for career day. He handed out hundreds of brochures and the phone at his barn had not stopped ringing since. The answering machine was always full of inquiries at the end of the day and he was about to consider hiring office help. He was feeling a little swamped.

The spring camp was full and he was having to turn kids away. He took down names and numbers on a list and promised to call if he found time during the summer to offer another camp. He hadn't quite figured out how to do that yet. He'd have riders and horses in full training and a barrage of shows to prepare for and he couldn't put much more on Miguel. Cleaning stalls, grooming horses and tacking them up for lunging and training kept Miguel constantly busy. He was going to have to add an extra barn hand.

Katie and the Morning Moms, as they called themselves, were really enjoying their time at the barn. The word had spread, however, and he had enough Moms interested to start another group. He was afraid to ask Katie for more of her time. He wasn't sure Roth wanted to give her up that much.

Plus, he needed his beginning lesson horses back. When the middle school kids took the brochures home, he had calls from parents wanting beginning lessons for not only middle school students but for elementary age kids, too.

Roth came over with Kaye and Katie on Thursday night to watch his ladies ride and drive. "This is too much fun, Mark," Roth smiled and folded his arms over his chest, raring back and showing how pleased he was with both ladies' performances.

"Yes, it's fun, but it's a lot of work, Roth. I have so many people wanting lessons right now that I can't handle it all anymore. Sure appreciate you letting Katie do the Morning Moms."

"She loves it, Mark. She's always been a very contented lady, but don't know when I've seen her this happy. Involvement here has been good for her."

"I'm glad. But I've got to figure out how to expand the operation. I just can't meet all the requests and needs anymore. Okay ladies, bring your horses in, that's enough for tonight." Mark instructed Kaye and Katie to return their horses. Miguel took Katie's horse and then they all walked back to the stall while Kaye took Stoney's tack off and gave him a rub down.

"Mark has been telling me about having more business than he can handle lately," Roth informed Katie and Kaye.

"Really, Mark? How so?" Kaye inquired. Mark told the three members of the Mason family what he was hoping to be able to do.

"So, Mark, what you're saying is: You need someone to do another Morning Moms' class."

"That's right, Kaye," Mark answered. "Plus, I could hold lots of camps this summer if I had more help. I'm going to have to hire more people."

With raised eyebrows, Roth asked, "Katie, do you think you could handle one more Morning Moms' Class?"

"Let's talk about all of this on the way home," Katie suggested. "Maybe we can come up with some ways to help Mark."

"I'd appreciate any suggestions you might have, Miss Katie, but don't you feel obligated to teach another class."

Katie smiled, turned to Roth and Kaye and said, "Come on you two. Let's go. I'll give it some consideration, Mark."

Chapter 17

On the way home Katie tried to discern how Roth would actually feel about her teaching a second Morning Moms' Class. Then she said, "Roth, you're not all that busy now. Mark has an outdoor arena. What if you helped out with some lessons?"

Roth looked at her with an expression that made Katie feel like she proposed he drive a rocket ship to the moon, and then said, "He hasn't asked me."

"Roth, we said we'd try to come up with some solutions to help the boy. Don't you want to be a part of it?"

"Just hadn't thought about it, Katie."

"You know he'll need help tacking up horses. You could assist Miguel. Drive the chuck wagon on the day he has the cookout. Help corral kids. I bet there's a hundred ways you could help."

Kaye chimed in with, "How about it, Grandpa?"

"What about you, Kaye? Couldn't you do a little work, too? You'll have spring break free. And what about this summer after you get that wedding and honeymoon out of the way? You'd be a great beginning instructor. You handled Stoney really well tonight."

"I don't know, Grandpa. Let's rest on it tonight and think some more in the next few days." *Besides,* Kaye was thinking, *I'm not sure how Tom will feel about this. I did go on a date or two with Mark before Tom and I became exclusive.*

March came in like a lamb and the days were becoming slightly warmer. If April showers truly brought May flowers rather than floods, Kaye was looking forward to spring. The days were windy just like March should be, but no severe weather was being forecast.

The day for the deposition did roll in with the wind picking up during that first week of the month. Chris had met with Mr. Brown and, through Arnold learned that Brown was a stepbrother of one of the main senior partners in the firm. This particular partner was not easy to approach. When Chris had attempted to explain why he shouldn't handle the case, he was met with, "You mean you can't handle a few questions with a few school personnel?"

Chris had assured the senior partner that he could, but wasn't looking forward to facing Kaye. He and Kaye had parted civilly when they were both stranded in Lexington during the ice storm, so he hoped everything would go well.

In order for the school system not to be put in a position to spend extra funds to hire a substitute teacher to cover Kaye's class, it was agreed (upon Kaye's request) that she could be the last one on the schedule to be questioned. That would have her appointment to give her deposition scheduled after school hours. She realized that she wasn't paid by the hour and would receive no extra compensation for the time she was spending outside the teachers' contract days, but she would rather donate the time than leave her class with a substitute when it wasn't, in her opinion, necessary.

Kaye finished up the day and went in search of Mrs. Adams and the principal to find out what to expect. She had a few minutes before she had to appear at the courthouse. Mrs. Adams and the principal had gone earlier and reported that CPS workers were being questioned now and that Kaye would be next. They said it wasn't bad and that neither one of them could say much as they had not had any reason to have very much contact with Cammy Jo. The child did not appear to need counseling and was not a discipline problem. They both felt their additions to the deposition were a waste of time. They didn't see how what they said would profit either side all that much.

Tom had offered to come and drive Kaye to the courthouse but she said it wasn't necessary. She had been instructed by the principal as to which room was being used. Since Mr. Brown was being represented by out-of-town counsel for some reason, they had agreed to use a small room at the courthouse rather than meet at the county attorney's office.

When Kaye was told to enter the room, the attorney assigned to Mrs. Brown smiled at Kaye and she thought she recognized the lady.

"Miss Mason, have a seat. This shouldn't take up too much of your afternoon and thank you for coming."

"Really people. Did I have a choice?" Kaye looked questioningly at Chris.

"Not really. Miss Mason, you look familiar. Did you by any chance ride horses in competition when you were younger?"

"Yes, I did."

"Then that's where I remember you. I rode, too. Seems like a long time ago. My name is Jennifer Lancaster. I am the attorney assigned to Mrs. Brown. This is Mr. Wilshire, the attorney representing Mr. Brown. I hope we haven't inconvenienced you too much this afternoon."

Kaye looked at the clock thinking, *This is Tuesday and I'd rather be preparing to line dance with Tom.* But instead replied, "No inconvenience. This concerns Cammy Jo and nothing I could do for her welfare could ever be considered inconvenient. I just hope all this truly turns out to be in her and her siblings' best interest," and Kaye looked directly at Chris when she said that. He received the warning in the message and responded. "That's what we are all hoping for, Miss Mason."

Kaye only looked at him with no response thinking, *No, it isn't. What you want is to win this case.* She had no intention of informing this deposition committee that she had been stupid enough to have been once upon a time thinking of being happily ever after married to the jerk. She was beginning to realize what a fairytale life she had led up to that time.

Jennifer Lancaster seemed stuck on the horse stuff and Kaye was not finding the conversation, no matter if it was to ease the situation, to be helpful in allaying her frustration with the happenings of the moment. "Did you show last summer, Miss Mason? Seems like I saw you riding a horse with Mark Elliott's stable at our local show," Lancaster asked.

"Yes, that's right."

"That's why I remember you so well. I ride with another stable and rode against you. You beat me."

"Sorry about that."

"Oh, don't be. I had a good time. Are you still with Mark? I've thought about checking out his stables. They're a little closer to town than the one I'm using and I live here in town, so it would be more convenient for me. Do you like his instruction?"

Good grief, Kaye thought, *could we please stop this horsing around and get on with this deposition?* But instead she said, "He's very good and really busy right now. You should, however, make a point to go see what he has to offer."

"When do you ride with him?"

"On Thursday afternoons." *Gee,* Kaye thought, *I supposed I'd be answering questions related to Cammy Jo, not revealing things about my life that I really would rather not have people in this room knowing.*

"Well, I might mosey over there Thursday, see you ride, check out my competition for the summer, and check out Mark, too," Jennifer said, smiling at Kaye and attempting to ease what appeared to be an abundant amount of tension in the room. "Now let's see what Mr. Wilshire would like to know." *Finally,* Kaye thought, but she wasn't looking forward to answering Chris's questions.

"Kaye, uh, Miss Mason," Chris corrected himself. The other attorney picked up on the slip immediately and looked from Chris to Kaye with one eyebrow raised and the side of her mouth slightly twisted. She knew something wasn't quite right. Chris continued with, "Tell me about Cammy Jo. What is she like as a student?"

"She's an above average student with what appears to be a talent in the area of visual arts. She draws amazingly well for her age."

"Is she liked by her peers?"

"Yes. She's kind and sought after for friendship from her peers. She is always one of the first children selected to be on teams during my time with them at P.E."

"What about her physical health?"

"Cammy Jo is quite athletic. I haven't noticed any health problems."

"Does she eat well?"

"I suppose. I don't eat with the children, but she has a good time at lunch from what I have observed. She socializes well. I really haven't looked at her tray when I pick up my students so I can't really make comments about how well she does or does not eat."

"So you don't know if she eats everything or is a picky eater or appears to be hungry?"

"No, I haven't observed any of that. If there was a problem, however, I feel the lunchroom monitors would have said something to me."

"What about the child's hygiene? Does she appear clean?"

Here it comes, Kaye thought. "She isn't any dirtier than any of my other students, if that's what you're after." Kaye returned with a look at Chris that would--if this were any other case--cause him to launch a stream of questions.

"We're not 'after' anything here, Miss Mason, only trying to make sure the Brown children have all the advantages available to them."

And just what would that be? Do any of you in this room really know what would be in these kids' best interest? I'm with this child more hours in the day than any of you, and I admit that I don't know what is really best for this family and I don't think any of you folks waving your law books around do either. Mr. Wilshire, Kaye thought, *you had all the advantages in the world. Private schools, law school and I can't tell that it helped you all that much. You're still a butthole. Come on, Kaye. Get hold of yourself and get your mind back on Cammy Jo.* She recognized that she was letting her feelings about Chris taint what she was saying and the way she was saying it.

"Are her clothes washed and does she have good shoes."

Boy, you are not going to leave anything out, are you, Chris? Kaye swallowed before answering because she wanted to say, '*Yes, but her mother's aren't. Mr. Brown will not let Mrs. Brown have her clothes.*' But she knew better than to go there. This was about the children--not about Mrs. Brown

"Her clothes are reasonably clean and her shoes fit." Kaye felt a little guilty here because Cammy Jo had complained about her feet one day the week before. It was a rather cold day and it had been raining. About mid-morning, when Kaye was circulating, checking math papers at the pupils' desks, she noticed Cammy Jo seemed uncomfortable. When she asked why, Cammy Jo said her feet hurt. Kaye had asked, "What's wrong? Let me see." The tennis shoes were wet and the child's feet were terribly red. Alarmingly so!

Kaye took the child's socks and shoes and set them on the register of the heater to dry out. That resulted in several pairs of shoes being set on the register. Kaye dismissed this as: give one child attention and you pay; then the others will demand the same amount. She remembered thinking and joking with her students that her room would soon become known as the 'stinky feet room'.

"Cammy Jo's social worker said she had purchased some medication to help with a condition with Cammy Jo's feet. Are you aware of the condition?"

"No one has informed me of any condition that I need to be aware of with Cammy Jo, so I am not." But Kaye knew the child's feet were really red and had an odor when she removed the shoes to dry.

"Have you seen where Cammy Jo lives?" Chris continued his query.

"I have not."

"So, you can't comment with any certainty about the living conditions?"

Whew! Kaye let out a small sigh and her chest didn't continue to feel quite so tight. Chris was letting her off. She didn't want to hesitate too long before answering so she said, "I have not seen where she lives," and let it go at that. Anything she'd heard would be hearsay, anyway, because she truly had not seen the property where the family was living. She'd let the social worker and the bus driver face those questions.

"That concludes the questions I have for Miss Mason," Chris informed the committee as he concluded his inquiry.

Jennifer Lancaster said, "Is there anything else you'd like to tell us regarding Cammy Jo, Miss Mason?"

"Only that she's the most delightful child I've ever known and I'd love to take her home with me and keep her forever."

"Well, sadly for you, Kaye, that's not going to happen. Seems she has two parents who want to hang onto her, too. But I'm glad she has you for a teacher." Jennifer Lancaster concluded the session by standing and offering a handshake to Kaye. The rest to the group stood and Chris extended his hand across the table to Kaye, holding it a bit too long and looking directly into her eyes while saying, "Thank you for coming."

Kaye said nothing just collected her things and went through the door thinking, *Where's the nearest restroom? I want to wash my hands.* But she stopped when she found the bus driver setting on the bench outside the room with a definite scowl on her face.

"Hi, Miss Mason. Isn't this a kicker! A real nice way to spend your afternoon! I don't get paid for this, you know, and I guess you don't either."

Payment was the farthest thing from Kaye's mind. This bus driver was really irritated. So Kaye wasn't the last one to be questioned that day after all.

"I should be home now taking care of my kids and fixing dinner for them and my husband. He isn't happy at all that I'm here after finishing my bus run instead of being at home."

Kaye wasn't sure how to respond so in the ensuing silence, the bus driver said, "What do they want to know? What was it like in there?"

"It's not bad," Kaye returned. The door opened and the bus driver was asked to enter the room. The driver and Kaye looked at each other with a frown and Kaye watched as the door closed behind the driver. Kaye's thoughts were, *Oh, no!* The question from Chris surfaced in her mind: "Have you seen where Cammy Jo lives?" and the driver would have to say, 'Yes.' Kaye knew what the following questions would be. "Would you comment on those conditions, please?"

Kaye hoped the driver wouldn't say it was a hell hole like she had said in the office back at school and that she would say that she could only comment about the conditions outside the home--not the inside. But Kaye knew the social workers had been inside the home and would have plenty to say about what they had witnessed--with windows out during freezing temperatures, and gosh knows what else. Kaye had to wonder where on earth Mrs. Brown had been to meet the two brothers where she was living. There were a lot of unanswered questions in this case.

Then it occurred to Kaye that not a single question had been asked about Cammy Jo's happiness. If she had been Jennifer Lancaster, she thought she would have asked, "Does the child appear to be happy?" She would have answered that the only time she had seemed tense or even a little bit anxious was when her dad had come to school with her backpack.

But how much would that have counted anyway? It was only a conjecture on her part and would probably be objected to and stricken from the records if she said that in a courtroom. Kaye realized that Lancaster probably knew what she was doing a lot better than she did. But a knot, about the size of a ball a child would use to play jacks, started slowly rising up her esophagus and seemed to lodge in her throat. Tears surfaced as she acknowledged the terrible feeling she had--that she was going to lose Cammy Jo. Maybe she needed to find a way not to get so attached to her students. But how could she help it, Cammy Jo was Cammy Jo, and who could resist her? She was someone Kaye didn't want to have to give up. Someone she wanted to follow with interest for the rest of her life. She felt a little sick knowing that her desire would probably be just that-- only a desire--and she had to prepare herself to let Cammy Jo go.

Tom picked Kaye up for their dance lesson to find a quiet partner who kept missing steps and turning the wrong direction in the line of dance. Her concentration was clearly not on learning this new dance.

He had asked about the deposition while riding in his truck on the way over to the Silver Saddle. Kaye had said it went all right, and then looked out the passenger side window. He continued with, "And Chris? How is Chris?"

Kaye turned and looked at Tom and said only one word, "Professional." Tom wasn't sure exactly what Kaye meant. But decided it wasn't good, and that as moody as Kaye appeared to be, that maybe he should drop the subject for the time being.

They made their way back to their table and after sitting for a moment, Kaye said, "Would you mind if we left a little early tonight? My mind just isn't here."

"I can tell. Let me help you into your coat. You don't need a cold to go along with your bad mood," Tom observed.

"Sorry. I'm not very good company tonight."

"Let's talk when we get in the truck," Tom suggested.

Kaye thought, *How lucky I am to have a guy in my life who is willing to listen to my problems. I'm never going to let him go.*

Tom closed Kaye's truck door, then walked around and let himself in, started the truck to access the heater, but didn't put the truck in gear. "Tell me what has you so distracted and upset, Kaye," he coaxed.

"Tom, it's just that never in a million years would I have thought about being dragged into a custody case because I am a child's teacher. I know it's probably common, but it has just slammed me against a wall today. I mean, we study lesson planning and teaching techniques, but there's nothing in a college course to prepare you for all the social issues you'll face. First it was Cory. Now it's Cammy Jo, and you just want to start building brick walls around those kids so you can keep the rest of the world out and prevent it from hurting them."

"Well, you can't do that, Kaye. You aren't going to be able to protect your students from everything they are going to face, especially when you have no control over their home life."

"I know that, but if I could, I would."

"I know you would, Kaye. That's one of the reasons why I love you. Now let me get you home. You need a good night's sleep. The only thing I regret is that you won't be asleep cradled in my arms."

Kaye smiled and said, "Soon, Tom, soon."

Chapter 18

Wednesday morning Kaye woke to the smell of bacon sizzling in one of Grandma Katie's iron skillets. She found Grandpa Roth drinking coffee and reading the morning paper when she entered the kitchen.

"Morning, Kaye. How'd line dancing go?" Roth quizzed her.

"Not well. I'm afraid having to give that deposition was on my mind more than any dance steps."

"Oh, how'd that turn out? Was Chris a real butthole as usual?" Roth continued with his interrogation.

"Roth Mason! You stop that!" Katie chimed in, pointing a finger at her forthright husband. Katie, however, knew she was thinking the same thing herself; she just hadn't said it out loud.

"Chris was…" and Kaye hesitated but decided to stick with, "professional."

"Really?" Grandma Katie remarked. "Well, I'm glad to hear that."

"Grandpa, have you thought anymore about helping out at Mark's?" Kaye asked, more than ready to change the topic of conversation.

"I have, Kaye, and as long as it's only for spring break, I think it might be fun. It's been almost a year since my operation and I think I'm up to it now."

"Good. I'm glad to hear that," Kaye smiled and patted her grandpa on the shoulder and then accepted a plate of bacon and eggs from her grandmother.

"How about you, Kaye? What have you decided? Did you discuss it with Tom last night?" Roth wanted to know.

"No, I haven't decided and I didn't even think about that last night. After that deposition I'm afraid I wasn't able to think about much else."

"That's too bad," Grandma Katie added. "What do you think is going to happen to those children, Kaye?"

"I don't have a clue, Grandma. I just don't know. I know I'd sure hate to lose Cammy Jo."

"Well, maybe you won't," Grandma Katie tried to put some positive thinking into the situation.

"Kaye," her grandpa interjected, "why don't you invite Tom to come with us to Mark's stable Thursday night? We could go catch a hamburger together after you ride and Katie drives. We could go to the Cupboard, if that's all right with everyone. Tom might even be able to offer some suggestions to help Mark with his overcrowded schedule." Roth was thinking that if Tom had a chance to have some input, he might not find it objectionable for Kaye to work for Mark. One thing he knew for sure, he surely didn't want anything to get in the way of his granddaughter's marriage to Tom. That was something he really wanted to see happen. If he could see Tom's reactions, he thought he might be able to advise Kaye a little better as to whether she ought to help Mark out at his barn.

"I can ask him, Grandpa. I don't know what he could suggest for Mark, but I bet he'd enjoy seeing Grandma drive."

Mark felt really tired but he had the driving lesson with Katie and the riding lesson with Kaye to complete before he could call it a day. Thank goodness for Miguel. What would he do without him?

When the barn had been constructed years ago, a large room had been built off the area that now housed a small kitchen. It was quite a large room and Mark was sure that in years gone by it had served as a bunkhouse for farm workers.

Miguel had made the room his home. He had lived in the Hope Springs area for many years and had once had his own house. He had shared it with his wife. They had not been able to have children. His wife, Rosa, had died with cervical cancer several years ago. Miguel told Mark that living in his house with too many memories of Rosa just made him too sad. So, he sold the house and now counted Mark and his horses as his family. Mark knew that Miguel became a part of every family who housed horses at his barn. He was just an easy guy to get along with.

Tonight, Miguel was taking a lady named, Jennifer Lancaster on a tour of the barn while Mark worked with Kaye and Katie. The barn was full tonight. Several of his clients were bathing their horses after their workouts and getting them ready for the night.

The hum of hair driers could be heard as Mark insisted that clients dry their horses before putting on their blankets to keep them warm against the nighttime chill. Most of those horses were body-clipped to keep them from sweating too much during their workouts. In cold weather, all that sweat was bad. If they were allowed to keep their winter coats, they could get wringing wet during a workout, then could possibly catch colds and pneumonia too easily. They needed to be body-clipped to prevent that from happening. But then without a winter coat of their own to protect them from the cold, they had to be blanketed. Spring was on the way and Mark was looking forward to not having to worry with strapping on blankets anymore.

Roth had come back to watch the lessons tonight and Tom was with him. This surprised Mark a little, but he learned that they would all be going out for a hamburger at the Cupboard afterward. He thought maybe that accounted for Tom's presence tonight--not that he had come only to watch Kaye ride Stoney.

Jennifer Lancaster was a pleasant distraction. Mark knew she was an attorney. He was fairly sure he had heard that she worked in the county attorney's office as an assistant. He would welcome her as a client if he could fit her in somewhere. He wondered if she owned her own horse. He'd have to find time to talk to her after these lessons. Miguel had completed his tour of the barn with her and had brought her into the ring where Kaye was riding Stoney. Katie was finishing driving Secret in the adjacent indoor ring.

Jennifer looked at Stoney and said, "He's a small horse, but he has wonderful action."

"Sure does," Mark agreed. "He can lift those legs like the big boys. But what is even better, he does it so smoothly. He makes it easy to maintain a good seat."

"Kaye, let's try some pattern work tonight. Are you up to it?" Mark asked loudly so she could hear him where she was riding on the outer edges of the ring.

"I guess," Kaye returned, looking at Jennifer Lancaster and thinking *I'd really rather not. If I can't do this, I get to look like a fool in front of another attorney.*

"Okay," Mark started issuing instructions and pointing said, "Start at this end of the barn, trot halfway down this side. Stop. Pick up your canter and canter a full circle and a quarter around the other end, stop at that end of the barn. Pick up your trot, come down the other side of the barn, cross over the center of the barn to the other side remembering to change your posting when you pass through the center, stop at the end of the barn where you started."

Kaye looked at him and finally said, "WHAT?"

"Want me to repeat that?"

"Please," Kaye confirmed. "That's a lot to remember."

Mark repeated the instructions. Kaye knew every eye in the barn was on her. Several clients who had finished grooming their horses for the night had gathered in the doorway leading back to the stalls.

Kaye had never competed in any shows requiring pattern work, but had many lessons as a child where instructors had her to ride patterns. She stopped Stoney and repeated the instructions aloud to Mark who confirmed she remembered everything correctly. Then she swallowed and began the drill. She didn't master it on the first try. Partly because it had been a while since Stoney had been worked in any pattern and partly because she wasn't real clear in giving directions to the horse. But on the second attempt, both the horse and the rider executed the ride beautifully.

She brought Stoney into the center of the ring, announcing, "That's enough for tonight."

"You did great, honey," Tom replied.

"Good job," Mark agreed.

"I'm impressed," Jennifer Lancaster said, with much admiration.

Miguel stepped up and took Stoney. "I'll put him up, Miss Kaye."

"Thanks, Miguel," Kaye said, appreciating the offer.

"I don't know about the rest of you, but here comes Katie. I guess she's got Secret put away for the night and I'm in need of that hamburger. Come with us, Mark," Roth extended the invitation.

"I think I better stay here, Roth, and talk with Miss Lancaster."

"Bring her along and talk to her over a hamburger, Mark. We can tell her all about you," Roth said in his mockingly, teasing way.

"I am sure you could and would, Roth," Mark responded with a smile.

"Do you have time, Miss Lancaster?" Mark asked.

Jennifer looked at Kaye and knew the feelings between them were a little awkward due to the Brown children's custody case. She said, "I think I should pass, Mark. I've seen enough to know my horse would be in good hands with you here in your barn. Miguel seems like a delightful person and very capable. Could I call you tomorrow and discuss fees?"

"Sure thing. You might get my answering machine. Just leave your phone number and I'll get back to you, probably late tomorrow after all lessons are completed."

"That will be fine, Mark. It was nice to meet all of you."

"You, too," everyone almost responded in unison. Jennifer smiled and walked out to her car. She was famished and decided to drive into town and grab something to eat at the Cupboard rather than having to fix something when she got home.

Mark decided to go with Tom and the Mason family and enjoy some down time even if it was only for a hamburger at the Cupboard. He really needed to get away for a while and then he was looking forward to a good night's sleep.

Coming through the door to the café, the first thing Kaye saw was Jennifer Lancaster giving the waitress an order. *Will I never be rid of attorneys in my life?* was Kaye's thought.

They scooted some tables together and invited Jennifer to join them. "I don't want to intrude," Jennifer apologized. "I didn't stop to think that you folks might be coming here."

"You're not intruding. Join us," Roth offered. So Jennifer transferred to the table, sitting next to Mark.

Everyone studied menus but ended up ordering the same thing—a burger and fries. Jennifer felt even more out of place when the waitress delivered her chef salad.

"That's what I should have ordered and saved some calories," Grandma Katie lamented.

"Oh, but you have been working with horses tonight. You probably burned off enough calories to justify eating a burger," Jennifer said in a consoling way.

"Grandma, your figure's perfect. Don't fret one minute about it," Kaye added.

Introductions had been made, but Jennifer Lancaster was not aware of how everyone was related. When she asked, Roth made her aware that he and Katie were Kaye's grandparents and Tom was Kaye's fiancé. "As far as Mark, he's on his own. Not related to this group at all, but we consider him almost a family member," Roth added.

"Congratulations! When's the wedding?" Jennifer inquired of Kaye.

"My parents will be coming to my grandparents' farm in two weeks and we will nail down the date then," Kaye informed her. "It's spring break and we'll be finalizing our plans."

"Oh, that's right. Mark, let's talk about your riding camp for spring break," Grandma Katie suggested. "Roth, why don't you tell him what we discussed?"

"I'm anxious to hear," Mark replied.

"Well, Katie has said she'd do your driving lessons. She suggested that I come along and assist Miguel with getting horses ready and maybe helping with the chuck wagon on your trail ride," Roth explained.

"That would be wonderful!" Mark said, almost collapsing his head into his hands. "I have some kids who ride with me all the time who are willing to assist, too. This should work out well. I have to admit, that for a few days lately, I have been thinking that I bit off more than I could chew with this camp. But if you folks are helping out, I might survive."

Jennifer was watching and listening and inquired, "You're having a riding camp during spring break? I assume this is for young people."

"Yes," Mark confirmed, "Katie has been helping out at the barn one morning a week with a group of ladies we call the Morning Moms. She's teaching them to drive. So she'll help with the young students teaching them to drive during camp."

"So what will these kids be doing at your camp, other than learning to drive?" Jennifer added to her list of questions.

"I really haven't worked it all out yet. But here's what I see so far. See what you all think and offer suggestions. I've helped with camps in other barns, but they had a lot more people than I do working for them. And I have to admit, I'm a little nervous about being able to pull all this off, even with the outside help I am going to be getting," Mark admitted.

"Oh, you'll do fine, Mark. Now tell us your plans so we can see how to help you," Katie assured and offered him.

"Okay, I was going to start around 10:00 AM. I know most camps start earlier, but I was trying to avoid feeding a bunch of kids breakfast."

Kaye's evaluation of this was, "Bad idea." That turned heads a bit, but she continued with, "What about parents who are still working during spring break? They can't leave work to bring a kid to you at ten o'clock."

"That's true," Jennifer added confirming Kaye's evaluation of Mark's plan.

"Tell you what, you have a kitchen in your barn, Mark. How about I shop and get things that kids eat for breakfast, something that's easy like cereal, fruit and donuts. Do you have a toaster in there?" Katie asked.

"Yes, a four slice job," Mark affirmed.

"Good. I'll get bread for toast, some butter and bring some of my homemade jam. Then we can offer milk, juice, and make hot chocolate. You have a microwave?" Katie continued to quiz Mark as she sized up the accommodations at Mark's barn.

"Got one of those, too." Mark added.

Katie finished with, "Okay, we're all set for breakfast. I'll come each morning at 7:30 and get everything ready."

"Well, I guess your start time and breakfast plans have all been altered," Roth reared back in his chair with a big grin and Tom suppressed laughter. Tom could tell that living in this family was definitely going to be interesting. He was going to enjoy seeing how they would plan the rest of Mark's camp and then wondered if they would be planning the rest of his life as well. His next thought was with all their help, however, that might not be such a bad thing.

"What's next, Mark?" Katie asked. "I need to know how you have decided to schedule the lessons if I'm going to teach driving. Then Kaye can work with me on how to structure the lessons I will be giving."

Mark responded with, "What comes to my mind might be a little different each day. I plan to divide the kids into two groups. I thought I'd leave horse care and putting harness and saddles and bridles on up to Miguel, but there's a little problem there. If he demonstrated harnessing a horse for your group, he can't demonstrate saddling and bridling for my group. There's only one Miguel."

"That's true," Katie agreed. "Here's where you could help, Roth. Goodness knows you know how to saddle a horse."

"Would you, Roth?" Mark asked excitedly. "I hadn't asked you to help because I didn't know if you were up to it or not after your surgeries."

"Oh, I reckon I can," Roth acquiesced.

"Great!" Mark was beginning to get excited. "This way, we can break into two groups. While Katie and I clean up the kitchen from breakfast, Miguel and Roth can demonstrate saddling and harnessing, then hand the two groups off to us to teach riding and driving. The kids have been instructed to bring their own lunches. You know, brown paper bag it. After lunch we'll have a lecture on different aspects of the horse and its care."

"Well, Mark, this camp of yours is really taking shape. You have day one planned. I want to hear what you're going to do for day two and thereafter. Can you do a whole week?" Tom asked.

"Sure can," Mark assured him. "Day two the kids start practicing harnessing and saddling. Then they start riding and driving. Day one will be mostly demonstrations. There will be another lecture on day two after lunch and probably time for another ride and drive session after the lecture. We want to make sure each kid gets a turn to actually be on a horse or be driving in a buggy. Days three and four we will switch groups. The group that learned to drive in the morning will learn to saddle and ride in the afternoon. The group that rode in the morning will practice driving skills in the afternoon. Day five will be field trip day. We are going to a veterinarian's clinic and to another barn. I'll need some help with transportation, but one of my clients has a van and has agreed to assist."

"Some of us can drive, too," Roth offered.

"Thanks, Roth. Day six is the grand finale. We'll ride and drive in the morning in kind of a small show to demonstrate to parents what the kids have learned during the week. That afternoon, we'll go for a trail ride with the parents loaded on a wagon for a hayride behind us. The guy who has my lesson horses is bringing them back to me for the week. They trail safely, as well as being good horses for me to teach beginning riding lessons. Thought I'd take one of my hay wagons back to a cleared spot near a pond on the property I am leasing and have a kind of chuck wagon feast in the late afternoon. They can fish in the pond, too. I have a place to tie the horses. I'll take a grill back there and do hotdogs and chips. Something not too complicated."

"Could Kaye and I help out with that?" Roth asked. "You'll be off that week, won't you Kaye?" Roth looked at Tom for his reaction, but Kaye more than took care of the moment.

"I can, if Tom will help. He's great with a grill and hotdogs. I know, I saw him do it at a picnic I helped him with for his Little League team," Kaye looked at Tom with questioning eyes.

"I think it would be a fun way to spend a Saturday afternoon," Tom said, agreeing to his assignment.

"Mark, you seem to have all this very well in hand," Jennifer commented. "It's great to see everyone pitching in. How much does your camp cost? I'm sure this isn't a free service you are providing."

"Oh, no. Wish I were well off enough to do it for free. I'm sure there are kids who can't afford to come. The price is $250 for the week and I am really cheaper than a lot of other barns that offer camps," Mark informed Jennifer.

"I can't help in any other way, but could we locate a kid who can't afford this and let me pay for their week? I'd be more than glad to do that," Jennifer offered.

Kaye and Tom looked at each other and Tom asked, "What's the age group, Mark?"

"Middle school."

"Kaye, what about Jason, your student, Cory's brother?" Tom suggested.

"That's perfect, if he's interested in horses. We know he loves playing ball," Kaye added.

Tom said, "Tell you what, I'll call his mother and see. She knows me from him being on my Little League team."

"Thanks, Tom. Just call the county attorney's office and let me know. I'll get the money to Mark as soon as you let me know," Jennifer instructed.

"Oh, is that where you work, Miss Lancaster?" Katie asked.

"Yes, I work there pro bono on a few cases, but mostly I work the cases in my own practice," Jennifer explained.

Kaye was thinking about children in elementary school and how much some of them would love to ride and benefit from the association with a horse. She asked, "Have you thought about a camp for younger kids, Mark?"

"I have, Kaye, but I'd need a lot more help with that age, kiddo, plus, I'd have to wait until summer to schedule it. And to be honest with you, I'm not sure I could handle it during show season even if some of my older students helped out. The older ones wouldn't be in school then and could help, but younger kids pose a greater risk around horses, as you would well understand since you spend most of your day with them. I would surely need an adult to supervise the older kids while they helped with the younger ones. Oh, gee, that is a lot of responsibility."

"Well, Mark, let us get through the camp for spring break and then we can talk about how to let some of Kaye's little ones have a camp. If we plan it for later in the summer, she might be back from a honeymoon then and she and Katie could help you with that," Roth suggested, keeping an eye on Tom's reaction again.

Tom seemed neutral, but Katie said, "Just a minute, Roth Mason. Before you go volunteering the two of us, we will want to hear what your contribution will be."

"Okay, Katie, I know I won't get off Scott free here, but like I said, let's get through spring break and see how we all do. Mark might not ever want any of us back in his barn again after that week," Roth suggested with a big laugh and patted Mark on the back since he was sitting on the other side of him from Jennifer Lancaster.

The plates of hamburger and fries arrived and everyone dived in. Tom and Kaye left together and Katie and Roth said goodnight to Mark and Jennifer, who stayed and discussed fees for boarding and training her horse. It was agreed that Mark would go pick up the horse the following day and Jennifer could start her lessons the next week. He would see if Kaye would mind sharing her lesson time with Jennifer. He thought riding with each other would be good for both ladies. After all, in a tournament or a show, they would be in the ring with lots of other riders.

Chapter 19

The weather was now at temperatures that didn't require anything but a light coat and Kaye had ceased to be worried about Cammy Jo freezing during the cold Kentucky nights. Other worries about Cammy Jo, however, seemed to be eminent.

Cammy Jo's mother had come to visit Kaye at school one afternoon and told her that when school was out she would be returning to her husband and moving to Lexington with him. She said she had no alternative, as not doing so would mean that she would have to challenge Mr. Brown in court for the custody of their children. She feared that he would have a better chance of winning than she would since she had no means of support and he did. So, in order to keep her children, she was going to go back to him.

It was Kaye's hope that this would be the best thing for Cammy Jo, but she really doubted that it was the best thing for Mrs. Brown. Kaye had to face the possibility that she would probably never again have any contact with Cammy Jo after the school year ended. That possibility had the effect of feeling like someone was reaching in her chest and wringing tears right out of her heart.

Spring break did, however, finally arrive. The kids were ready for a break and so were the teachers. Kaye looked forward to the week without having papers to grade or kids to supervise. Her weekend would be spent with her parents and grandparents finalizing wedding plans. She would be working a little with Mark at his camp, but it wasn't the same as being responsible for twenty-four children for six hours everyday five days a week.

Jean and Bill were on their way in from Paducah. Jim Johnson had agreed to close up the hardware store for them on Friday night so they could get an early start. Jean was developing more and more faith in Jim's ability to manage the store and admitted to Bill that she was feeling a lot calmer about turning the management of the store over to Jim so that she and Bill could semi-retire.

But this weekend, Jean was not going to think about the store or retirement or any of those life-draining activities that seemed to tug at your tired mind. She was looking forward to the buzzing activity around finalizing the plans for her daughter's wedding. There really wasn't a whole lot that was yet to be done.

They had already talked by way of the phone and discussed most everything that needed to be completed. It was finally decided to have the reception at the Tollhouse Restaurant. The construction on the party room was nearly completed and the young couple that owned the place was delighted to be able to accommodate the Mason family by having the wedding at their new facility. They said they would even work with the caterers and see if they could add anything to the festivities from their menu. Jean thought this was more than kind since she had already hired the caterer before they had decided to have the reception in the new part of the Tollhouse restaurant.

Kaye and Jean would make a visit to the restaurant on the weekend and check out what decorations they might need. Jean was going to suggest that they have another mother-daughter weekend together to go and select those items.

Invitations were selected and the only thing the printer needed was the date so he could enter it on the card. Then there would be another weekend for sending them out. The group had a mailing date of the first of May so that everyone would have time to put the June wedding date on their calendars.

Kaye and Jean had spent the previous weekend looking for the perfect wedding dress. Even after trying on several different dresses, and visiting three different cities to do it, Kaye was not satisfied that she had found the right dress to go with her great-grandmother's veil. Even though it had been fun seeing Kaye in all those pretty dresses, Jean was getting a little worried. But Kaye assured her she would settle on something soon.

Saturday brought a flurry of activity. Kaye found that there was so much activity floating around in her brain that she was talking to herself. *Dates, dates, dates! How will I keep up with all of this? There's so much going on at school and in my personal life. Will I be able to do all of this? Okay, Kaye, take a deep breath. You can do this.*

But before she had left school on Friday, she noted one more date. It concerned Cammy Jo. Her birthday was coming up on Thursday of spring break.

By noon, the wedding committee had settled upon the third weekend in June for the date of the wedding. The printer was notified. He told them that he was working and could actually have the invitations ready in about two hours if they wanted to pick them up. Jean, Grandma Katie, and Kaye were delighted. The printer was local and they decided to work one more hour, take a break and have lunch in Hope Springs before making a visit to the printer.

They finished up with orders for napkins since the date was now available to be printed on them. The cake and colors had already been selected. Tom's tuxedo was rented. They called the lady everyone in Hope Springs used to make bride's maid dresses and scheduled an appointment with her at 4:00 PM. Then the three of them headed off to lunch in Hope Springs.

As promised, the printer was true to his word and had the invitations all boxed up and ready to go when they entered his shop. Across the street from the shop was a second-hand store.

Kaye was almost mesmerized at the display in the window. Jean had to grab her elbow to keep her from stepping into the street and getting hit by an oncoming car. "Kaye, forever more! What is wrong with you?" her grandmother asked. "You can't be a much of a bride if you get yourself smashed flatter than a pancake in the middle of the street."

"Oh, Grandma! Look! Look in the window across the street!" All three women looked at a mannequin in full bridal regalia. Kaye handed her keys to her mother saying, "Mom, I left great-grandmother's veil in a box in my truck. I haven't taken it in since our trip last weekend. Get it out, please."

Jean did as instructed and the ladies made their way across the street, a little more carefully this time. Kaye certainly didn't want anything happening to that veil.

When they entered the store, the proprietor asked if he could help and Kaye explained that she was interested in the wedding dress. "That's a real bargain. They only want one-hundred dollars for it." Kaye and Jean just looked at each other. After the price tags they had experienced last weekend on a number of the dresses Kaye had tried on, they couldn't believe their ears. "It will take me a minute or two to get it off the mannequin. I do suppose you want to try it on. There is a dressing room in the back with a mirror and everything. What do you have in the box?"

"It's my great-grandmother's veil that she wore in her wedding. I have been searching for the perfect dress to go with it and who would have thought I'd find it right here in Hope Springs?"

Grandma Katie smiled and added, "The old saying is 'look right in your own backdoor first'. It usually works. After all that is where you found Tom."

While the storeowner struggled to get the mannequin out of the window and undress her, Kaye was holding her breath and praying the whole time that he wouldn't damage the dress. When he laid the dress in her arms, she looked at her mother and grandmother and said, "If this dress doesn't fit, I'm going to cry."

"Oh, don't! It really does look like it is just your size," her mother consoled.

When Kaye emerged no one spoke. Grandma Katie picked up the veil and placed it on Kaye's head. The combination was perfect and the dress was not even going to need one stitch of alteration. Everyone but the storeowner was on the verge of tears.

"Well, what do you say? Do you want me to bag it for you?"

Kaye turned to the mirror and answered, "Without a doubt, please do."

The ladies emerged from the secondhand store looked at each other and Jean burst out laughing. "We must have some fun with this with your father. Let's put off telling him how much we've spent. I actually can't wait to tell him the bride's maid dresses are probably going to cost more than the wedding gown. A hundred dollars! Can you believe this?" All three ladies had a huge group-hug right there on the sidewalk before crossing the street to Kaye's car. The storeowner looked outside and smiled and then began searching for another outfit to cover his very naked mannequin.

The trip to the seamstress came next and fabric and patterns were considered. Selections were made and Kaye suddenly had an idea. There were no little children in their family for the flower girl. Cammy Jo immediately came to her mind. She wondered if Cammy Jo's father would arrange for Cammy Jo to be brought back to Hope Springs for the wedding. She suspected they would be whisked off to Lexington as soon as school ended. Mrs. Brown had said that Mr. Brown had agreed to leave the children where they were until they finished this year of school.

Kaye also had to choose a ring bearer. There were no little boys in her family either and none of her friends had kids old enough to perform the task, other than Julie and Jerry Mayhugh and she wasn't sure their little boy was old enough to perform the task successfully.

If she was going to use Cammy Jo for the flower girl, why not let Cory be the ring bearer. The only fear she had was that she would make the other children in her class jealous. Surely there had to be a way to do this and keep it under wraps until the actual wedding. If she could do that, her students would be moving on to a new teacher the next year and maybe she could avoid the fact that she was kind of 'playing favorites' as she had heard the term expressed so many times.

Kaye started up the conversation concerning using the two students with her mother and grandmother and the seamstress, Mrs. Evans, couldn't help but overhear. "Could I be allowed to suggest something, Kaye?" the seamstress interjected. "Are you going to invite your students to the wedding?"

"I had not thought of that, but I suppose it could be done." Kaye admitted.

"Okay, just ask the parents to dress the children in nice clothes and equip each one with soap bubbles. They put them in tiny little jars, just to be used in weddings," Mrs. Evans added.

"Oh, yes. I saw them in one of the magazines," Jean confirmed.

Mrs. Evans continued with her idea. "See if this will work, Kaye. Give all the kids who attend a job. Let them form two lines, one on each side after the wedding has ended and you have finished with your reception line. Let only the kids have the little jars of bubbles and it will be their job to blow bubbles for you to exit the church or wherever it is you are to be married. If enough of them don't show up, get enough bubbles for all of your guest to have a bubble bottle. They are not too expensive. It's always good to have a back-up plan, and that way all the children can have a part in the wedding and that should help some with the jealousy issue." With that she completed her explanation.

Kaye, her mother and grandmother all thought this was an excellent idea, but if she singled out Cory and Cammy to be a bigger part of the ceremony, wouldn't that still present a problem? Her grandmother came up with a plan to help with this, but she waited until they all got back into the car before she revealed her plan.

"Kaye, I don't often encourage lies and deception, but I know you really want these two kids to be your ring bearer and flower girl, and I understand why you do, after all that you have witnessed them going through this year. Plus, I know you are concerned that you won't see Cammy Jo again after this school year ends, so see what you think about this. Put all the kids' names in a pot--boys in one, girls in the other--and do a drawing. Only, and here's the deceptive part, all the papers in the girls' pot will have Cammy Jo's name on them and the papers in the boys' pot will have only Cory's name on them. Then when you do the drawing you will have selected the two kids' names that you want."

"Oh, Grandma! I had no idea you could be so devious! But I think I could get away with it." Kaye excitedly considered what her Grandmother had proposed.

Then Katie explained, "I didn't want to say anything in front of the seamstress. I thought we better keep this one under wraps and just in the family."

Jean agreed, "Very good thinking, Katie."

"I'll have to put out a letter to my parents that will serve as an invitation for the children to come and participate. I think this will work. I will explain about the drawing and then get in touch with Mrs. Brown and Mrs. Wilson to see if they will permit Cammy Jo and Cory to be in the wedding."

"All right. I think we have this thing under wraps, Kaye, but if you will, let's stop by the drug store on the way home. I need to pick up some medications for Roth," Grandma Katie requested.

"Sure thing, Grandma," and Kaye backed her car out of Mrs. Evans's drive and headed for the pharmacy. While Katie got the prescriptions, Kaye and Jean browsed the store. On the school supply aisle, Kaye again remembered that Cammy Jo's birthday was coming up on Thursday. "Mom, could I ask you to do something for me?"

"Well, I guess so, Kaye, what is it you want?" Jean was curious to know.

"Thursday is Cammy Jo's birthday. She shows so much artistic ability. If I buy some art supplies and wrap them up could you mail them from Paducah? That way they will not have the Hope Springs post office mail stamp on them. It might not be as easy to figure out who sent them that way."

"Tell you what. I have to go to Lexington on Monday. What if I mail them from there?"

"Mom that would be perfect! It would maybe look, at first, as if her Dad bought them. His new job is in Lexington but I think I told you that. Of course, if questioned, he will inform them that he didn't buy the stuff, but I don't care. I would just like for her to have some nice art supplies. If she were my little girl, I would have her enrolled in art classes. She is that good. I just love to see the pictures she draws and colors."

"Kaye, we can't get really good stuff in this drug store. Let me go to a craft store in Paducah before I head to Lexington. There's a real good one that just opened up in the old downtown section, and they have good quality items. In fact, when I was in there last week they had a complete art kit--drawing paper, paper to use to paint, watercolors, two small sets of paint; one was oil, the other acrylic; plus they had a set of watercolors. There were all kinds of drawing pencils and a bunch of other stuff that I wouldn't even know how to use. It was only about fifty dollars. Since you think so much of this kid, why don't I just order it on-line? The store has a website. Then I can have them ship it to her. Tell you what, I'll even pay for half of it. I am looking forward to meeting the little lady. But you better have this drawing thing for flower girl and ring bearer soon if you want Mrs. Evans to do Cammy Jo's dress."

"I do. We can rent a small tux for Cory. Mom, you're too good. I absolutely love you."

"And I love you, too, Kaye. Maybe pretty soon you will have your own little girl to dress up and enroll in art classes."

"I hope so, Mom, but if you don't mind, I think I will wait at least a year or two."

"That's fine with me. Your Dad and I have been talking about retiring and maybe moving back here so we can be closer to Roth and Katie and help them out with some of their needs as they age. Plus, the thought had come to us that if we do move here, we'd be close to you and Tom and any grandchildren you might see fit to give us."

Kaye couldn't believe her ears. She looked at her mom, swallowed and said, "Do Grandma and Grandpa know about this yet?"

"Not yet. We haven't really started working on it too hard yet."

"Well, after having a moment to consider what you are saying, I think it is a wonderful idea, but what will you do with the store?"

"Jim Johnson is becoming very capable in handling everything. We would sort of semi-retire and let him buy the store. He could make payments on it and that would supplement our income for quite a while."

"You really *have* given this a lot of thought, haven't you, Mom?"

"Well, at first, Kaye, I wasn't too much for the idea. You can see that selling our house, building or buying another one here, overseeing the business from a remote location and getting involved in farm life with Roth and Katie are going to be big adjustments for both your father and for me."

At that moment Katie appeared armed with several bags of prescriptions. "What will be a big adjustment for you and Bill, Jean?" Katie asked.

"Oh, you have your drugs, I see. Let's get headed back. I think Bill wants to talk to Roth about our next few years. We are considering retirement, Katie."

"Oh, that does require some adjusting. Talk about retiring, sometimes I wish I could retire from cooking. If we had a Kentucky Fried Chicken in this town, this is one night when I would agree to take home a bucket of that stuff for supper. I really don't feel much like cooking tonight. I do have a ham I baked yesterday and we can slice some of that and find something else to go with it."

"Katie, I think Kaye and I can take care of supper. Do you still have jars of those canned pickled beets that you did and that Bill is always bragging about?"

"Yes, they are in the pantry."

"I bet you have plenty of potatoes, too."

"Oh, yes. Roth raised some good ones last summer, even while he was convalescing from that operation. There are a few left. Plus, I have some green beans that I put in the freezer. That should just about do it."

Kaye chimed in with, "Then supper is planned, except for biscuits and we do not have to have them. But if you will guide me, Grandma, I would love to learn how to make them from scratch."

"I can do that and will even volunteer to set the table if you two do the cooking and clean up."

"It's a deal." Jean sealed the conversation and the three ladies headed home with supper plans completed, and wedding plans almost complete. Kaye couldn't wait to see Cammy in a pretty little dress. The thought occurred to her, though, that the child had never been to school in a dress. Cammy was very athletic and might not want to wear a pretty little dress or to drop rose petals down the aisle of a church. Kaye thought she would cross that bridge later, if it were necessary.

Chapter 20

Monday of spring break rolled around and brought the first day of Mark's camp. Katie had breakfast for about a dozen middle school age kids. She was enjoying hearing their stories of school days and exploring hearing about their anticipation and expectations for the week of camp.

She found that none of them had ever driven a horse. That didn't concern her a lot. After all, they were here to learn. If they already knew how to drive, what would be the purpose of her teaching them?

She divided them into two groups and sent one group to Roth to learn about tack and how to saddle and bridle a horse. The other group was off to Miguel to learn about harnessing a horse and hitching it to a buggy.

That was followed by the saddle and bridling group going to Mark for a demonstration on riding. He went through proper mounting technique, how to hold the reins, and what to do to position your body for a proper seat on the horse. He explained that today they were expected to demonstrate that they could mount and dismount properly. Tomorrow they would be riding.

Mark demonstrated the techniques he had been teaching, ending his session with the students practicing mounting and dismounting the horse. He used two lesson horses for this practice session. The one he used for demonstration purposes of riding techniques was owned by Jennifer Lancaster and was a fairly stepped-up horse. The students really enjoyed seeing this horse, as it was capable of putting on quite a show. When he finished riding Jennifer's horse, Miguel took it and put it up and Roth brought out two very old and tolerant lesson horses named Ride On and Hop to It. Since neither horse was capable of living up to its name anymore they were perfect for the students to use in practicing proper mounting and dismounting.

The group that Miguel had taught to harness a horse was sent to Katie. She talked about getting in and out of the buggy safely, how to hold the reins and how to give right and left turning directions to the horse without harming the horse's mouth. Then she gave a driving demonstration followed by each student practicing getting in and out of the buggy safely.

They broke for lunch which Mark made interesting by doing little oral quizzes about what the students had learned that morning. He explained that tomorrow they would be expected to use what they had learned in order to proceed on to riding and driving.

The afternoon was spent first demonstrating how to groom a horse. Mark let each student come to the horse he was using and practice picking up its feet and holding a hoof pick in order to clean the horse's hooves. He explained the importance of keeping a horse's feet in good condition, ending with saying, "No foot, no horse." The students understood that this meant that you can't ride a lame horse. A horse needs good feet, properly cared for, in order to carry a rider safely.

After he finished, each student was issued a bucket of grooming equipment and sent to a stall where a horse was cross-tied and waiting to be groomed. Mark told everyone to do a good job because, for the next few days, they would be expected to groom their horses before getting them ready to ride and drive. He explained that by the end of the week, he expected everyone to be proficient in grooming. He also explained that the best grooming tool was a person's hand. He told them that after they finished with currying tools, cleaning brushes and finishing brushes, they should run their hands over the horse to make sure they had not missed any spots. He smiled and said, "Your hand is your evaluation tool as to how well you have performed the task of grooming."

The students left that day eager to return and actually get to ride or drive a horse the following day. Katie and Roth left feeling good about helping Mark and thoroughly enjoying seeing young people learn about horse care. Roth said, "It was Winston Churchill who said, 'There is something about the outside of a horse that is good for the inside of a man.' I say every kid ought to learn to ride and care for a horse. There would be a lot less of the meanness that goes on these days. Keep 'em busy doing something useful."

"I heard Mark say that one barn near here actually works with delinquent kids, Roth. He said the instructor in that barn gives a kid, who is out of control, a really mean horse and says, 'Now learn to control yourself so you can control this horse. Because if you don't, this horse will kill you.' Can you imagine? I mean, what if the kid really is obstinate and doesn't want to control a horse? I could see that actually becoming a deadly situation."

"I think I know who you are talking about, Katie. He does work with delinquent kids, but I think they have to have expressed an interest in horses before he takes them on. That probably keeps the kid from getting murdered. But horses can sense so much. They probably know what to do to straighten a kid out better than we do."

"I hope so. Do you remember when that lady visited our barn with her two little girls who were 'mentally challenged,' as Kaye would say? Remember Lady Red? She lowered her head over the rails of her stall so the girls could pet her. She wouldn't do that for anyone else. I could have sworn she knew about their condition."

"She probably did. We just do not have any way of communicating with her to find out. Well, Katie, my dear, tomorrow's another day. Are you ready to put some kids in a buggy and actually watch them drive?"

"Roth, my anxiety is climbing. I just hope no one gets hurt. Hopefully no buggies will get turned over, no one will fall off the back of the buggy and everyone will go home with happy tales to tell."

"They will, Katie. After all, look who they have for a teacher."

"I love you, Roth, but I think your confidence in me is higher than mine is."

"You'll do fine, Katie, my girl."

Day two of camp worked beautifully with no accidents. Students groomed the horses. One group practiced putting saddles and bridles on and the other group practiced harnessing the three horses that were being used for driving lessons. The groups rode or drove once before lunch and again following lunch. They went home full of pride with happy smiling faces and plenty to tell their parents.

Day three began with the groups switching. Roth and Miguel demonstrated harnessing and saddling and bridling to their new group. That meant Katie and Mark had switched groups and they did their demonstrations. The afternoon was followed by a lecture from Mark on proper care of tack. Each student was issued a saddle and bridle and had to clean it. Mark told them to make special note of how the bridle was assembled because they would have a little contest later concerning the assembly of a bridle.

The following day every student was able to groom his or her horse, saddle and bridle it or put harness on without assistance. They rode or drove once in the morning and once after lunch. Mark said he would save his lecture until after everyone had ridden, taken the tack off their horse and stored it in the tack room in its proper place.

He asked the students to return to the tack room in pairs, select a bridle and bring it to the room where he was holding lectures. He instructed them to study the bridles closely and then to leave them lying on the tables.

Friday was the day the students were to take a field trip to another barn. They were not due to leave for a couple of hours after arriving. So, after everyone had eaten breakfast, Mark took the group to the lecture room and asked that they pair up with the person they were with yesterday before they entered the room. When they went into the room, they discovered the bridles they had brought from the tack room yesterday had been disassembled. Mark explained that their task was to reassemble the bridles and the team who finished first would receive a free riding lesson after the camp ended.

Mark videotaped the students as they attempted to put the bridles back together. It all became rather hilarious, as they had no sample bridle from which to work. When time was called, no team had reassembled the bridle correctly. Mark then hung up a bridle that was put together correctly and let the students use it to assist them in correcting their mistakes. Each team ended up with a bridle that they could use.

Mark explained that this was a good thing because they would use those bridles tomorrow when they did their show for their parents. The rest of the day was spent going to another barn and seeing the horses that were being trained there. They went to a special farm where the owner had a collection of buggies. Some were real antiques and very beautiful. All of the students went home talking and laughing at how silly they appeared that morning trying to assemble those bridles.

Saturday was show day and Mark began the session with the video of the students trying to assemble the bridles and showing some of the things they did and saw on the fieldtrip. The parents were allowed to go into the barn and stand outside the stalls while the kids groomed and saddled their horses. Everyone got to ride today, only this was going to be a trail ride to the cookout.

Roth hitched up the team to the wagon, loaded the parents and took them bouncing along to the cookout site. They met Katie, Kaye and Tom there with hotdogs and hamburgers cooking. Katie had everything ready and the serving line moved along swiftly. No one wanted the day to end.

Katie didn't want the week to end. She could never remember a better time at a horse barn and she had ridden horses all her life. Before she left, Mark asked, "Well, Miss Katie, are you ready to attempt a camp for some younger kids this summer? I will have several older kids to help us with that camp?"

"I will surely give it some thought, Mark. I can't remember when I have ever enjoyed anything so much."

"That's great. The Morning Moms are so pleased with their lessons and you heard the parents today telling you about their kids coming home and talking about Miss Katie this and Miz Katie that. It had to make you feel good."

"It did, Mark. It surely did."

Roth didn't say a word. He just smiled. Once again his Katie had won everyone's heart. She had won and kept his for all these years and he was so glad it had been her. He had met a lot of women in his life, but none of them could have held a matchstick to Katie's ability to shine in his heart.

Chapter 21

Tom and Kaye drove over to his house following the cookout they had helped with for Mark's final day of horse camp. "Kaye, we only had today to observe Jason at Mark's. It was rather good seeing him there. I, like you, had worried about him and Cory after what they went through during Christmas break when their Dad went off the deep end again with his abuse of their mother. Then the breakup of their parents has had to be hard."

"I don't know, Tom. Cory has seemed to be more open to friendships and to talking to adults since his mother declared her independence. That had to take so much courage on her part."

"She had her parents nearby and that was a good thing."

"Yes, it was, Tom. But think about it. Would you want to have to rely on your parents to bail you out of a situation like that? I know I wouldn't," Kaye said looking out the passenger side window where she was sitting in Tom's truck.

"Oh, don't get too independent on me now, Kaye. I need to know that I, at the very least, am needed and can be with you to bail you out of anything you might come up against," Tom bantered back with a little smirk and a small laugh.

"What makes you think I am going to get into scrapes where I need you to rescue me?" Kaye looked across the truck with defense in her voice and a face that made Tom laugh even more.

"Really, Kaye, life is just like that. We all mess up at times and I hope you will be there to listen, help, and offer me advice.

If we can do that in our marriage, I believe it will survive forever. From what I have seen, it is when people do not talk to their spouse about problems they are having and go blabbering to someone else that causes a lot of the problems with couples these days." Tom said this with a lot of conviction and sincerity.

"You amaze me, Tom. You are right. If we can always talk like we have just now, I have no doubt that we will make it."

"We will and so will Cory and Jason. They have had a lot of support. I have to admit that I never knew school personnel would become so attentive to kids' problems like you guys have. It takes much more to be an educator that I could ever have realized."

"Well, Jason did have fun at the camp this week. Grandma Katie talked about him some and she said he just seemed to be a natural with the horses and the kid had never been around one before."

"I guess that's what it is all about. Mark is really beginning to offer some great things for kids. I actually had an idea about something he might add to his programs. See what you think, Kaye. What if he recruited some teachers, like you, who know about horses and had them to start horse clubs in their schools? They could be called Equine Education or something like that. You could do things at the school and things at his barn. That would pull more people in."

"Excellent idea! Why don't you suggest that to him? I think if it came from you, it would mean more than me suggesting it. By the way, you were great today at that cookout. The grill master extraordinaire!"

"Didn't Jennifer Lancaster put up the money for Jason to attend the horse camp?" Tom asked.

"Yes, she did. Jason's grandparents drove him to camp each morning. His mother was working and attending classes this past week. The college does not have spring break at the same time as the schools. Teachers who are going back to the university just don't get a spring break while they are working on their advanced degrees. They are usually stuck at home during spring break writing papers."

"Have you discussed any more plans for horse camps for younger kids this summer with Mark? I think he should do that."

"I did, but he is uncertain he can handle a camp like that with little kids. They require a lot more attention than those middle school kids. He has the show season in full swing at that time, too. There's a lot more activity at a barn like that in the summer. Older kids are out for the summer and coming to the barn almost daily taking care of their horses and training. Plus, there's the adult riders like Jennifer Lancaster, who own their own horses, and compete regularly."

"What do you think about Jennifer Lancaster? Think she and Mark might hit it off?"

"Who's to say, Tom? In matters of the heart, I place no bets."

"Good idea," Tom replied and patted Kaye on the knee.

"I'll tell you what I think is another good idea," Kaye added.

"What's that?"

"Well, Grandma, Mom, and I have nearly everything taken care of for the wedding. There's only one more item and I think you and I need to do that tonight."

"Yes. I'm listening," Tom assured her.

"Let's write those wedding vows."

"You're on," Tom said, pulling his truck to a stop at his old comfortable farmhouse. It was the perfect place to write.

Chapter 22

Monday morning brought an end to spring break and school took off with a vengeance. Spring testing was coming up and the tension was as taut as a banjo string. Kaye thought a lot of those taut, uptight strings might get broken before they could get the task of testing completed. Teachers' faces and eyes brought on a look as if they were having to deal with some kind of a plague. She really wished there were better ways to measure the accomplishments of students than a week of all the sit-quietly-and-follow-directions-to-a-tee, which the students had to endure.

The teachers found it taxing, too. There were no homework assignments or papers to grade in the evening, just a bunch of instructions to read through so that the teacher made sure he or she was conducting the test exactly like every other educator was supposed to be doing across the entire state. Kaye kind of wondered how that could even be possible. All the teachers she knew at Hope Springs Elementary, however, did endeavored to be as accurate and honest as possible.

She had to laugh when she remembered one of her middle school teachers administering those achievement tests to her class years ago when she was in eighth grade. She was pretty sure that what he did was an attempt to lessen tension, but he was a pretty funny guy, with a lot of dry sarcastic humor, who had no trouble telling anyone what he thought of the directions given to the teaching staffs for giving that test. Everything the teacher is to say on those tests is printed after the word **SAY:** printed in big black capital letters.

So every time he opened his mouth to give them directions he would say, "Say," and then proceed on with whatever it was he was being dictated to say. He had stated to the students that the people who wrote the test must think all teachers are imbeciles incapable of giving directions. All the students in his class thought this was hilarious, but Kaye doubted that her elementary age students would get that type of humor at all. Plus, as serious as everyone was about this test, she knew what repercussions she would face if she attempted something like that, and she never looked forward to a reprimanding lecture. Besides, middle school teachers and elementary teachers were breeds unto their own. It was sometimes funny to watch the interactions between the two groups when placed together. Their behavior sometimes reflected the age of the groups they taught. It wasn't that elementary teachers acted in any way immaturely, they just tended to be a little more coddling than middle and high school teachers. *But really,* Kaye thought, *those older students don't need mollycoddling, and would probably hate you for doing it.*

A fun part of the next week was explaining to the students about her wedding and the part she wanted them to play in it. She read the letter she wanted each one of them to take home with them explaining how she would choose the flower girl and ring bearer, leaving out, of course, that the drawing would be rigged. She left a space for parents to sign and to return so she could gage the response and hope that Cammy Jo and Cory's parents would return the letter.

They did and the drawing was held. Another letter was sent home announcing the results of the drawing. Kaye made arrangements to take Cammy Jo and Cory to the tuxedo shop and to the dressmaker the following Monday after school. Cammy Jo thought Cory looked like a penguin in his tux and Cory accommodated her laughter by walking like one across the fitting room floor. Kaye was having a ball with the two children as the parents had agreed for her to take them by herself to the seamstress and tux store. Then they would meet her at The Cupboard where they would all enjoy a meal together and discuss the wedding.

Kaye was rather shocked to see Mr. and Mrs. Brown enter the restaurant together. Mr. Brown played the perfect gentleman and husband, opening the door for Mrs. Brown, who was dressed in a very attractive set of slacks, with a matching cream colored silk blouse and a very expensive darker brown jacket and, much to Kaye's relief, a very nice pair of swede shoes that matched the outfit.

Try as she might, Kaye could not imagine the conditions that had to have occurred in that home to cause Mrs. Brown to leave and take her children to a place that was deplorable enough that the Department of Child Protection might consider taking them away from her. She realized, however, that the precise details of those circumstances would probably never be revealed to her. In these circumstances, Kaye was beginning to realize that she would probably never really be able to tell who was at fault. Both parties would claim the other one to be crazy and sometimes, it seemed like to Kaye, that maybe both of them were. At any rate, she had made the decision to never try to make a judgment about who was at fault or who was crazy. It really didn't matter. What Kaye was concerned about was how the children were being handled during all the turmoil.

So, she smiled and directed the couple to sit down. They had just been seated when Cory's mother and grandparents entered. Kaye was glad to see Mrs. Wilson. She feared she might not be able to make it, but she was informed that Mrs. Wilson had been given some time off from her job in order to meet Kaye and she didn't have classes tonight. Mrs. Wilson was looking a little tired, but she seemed to have a new, kind of relaxed, attitude.

Cory and Cammy Jo sat by each other and told the penguin story to their parents who looked on with smiling faces. Cammy Jo told her mother that she should see the pictures on the pattern of the dress being made for her, that it was really pretty. Remembering how athletic Cammy Jo had been all year during P.E., Kaye breathed a sigh of relief in hearing her say this. Perhaps

Cammy Jo had so many sides to her that she would constantly be full of delightful surprises to everyone who met her. She had certainly had that effect on Kaye. Cammy Jo would probably always be able to go from tomboy to little lady all her life.

Kaye told the parents and grandparents that she would be back in contact with them regarding picking up the clothing and the times for the rehearsals, as well as the time they would need to arrive for the actual ceremony. She also told Mr. and Mrs. Brown that Cammy Jo's dress would be ready for a fitting on Friday and could they please either come with her or pick her up after Kaye took her for the fitting. Her father said he would be in Lexington that afternoon, but Mrs. Brown assured Kaye that she would meet her after school and go with them to the fitting.

On Friday, Kaye and Cammy Jo left school with Mrs. Brown. Kaye drove as the two brothers who lived in the hollow had delivered Mrs. Brown to the school. She was in the same outfit that she wore to the restaurant on Monday night. Kaye surmised that her husband had allowed her to have at least one of her sets of clothing. Both Kaye and Mrs. Brown enjoyed seeing Cammy Jo in her dress, even though it still had to be hemmed and taken in a little on the sides. Cammy Jo was going to be adorable.

There was so much that Kaye wanted to ask Mrs. Brown, but felt she didn't have the right to intrude into the Brown's personal life. She wondered if Cammy Jo had received the art supplies that her mother had mailed to her from Lexington for her birthday. But she didn't dare risk letting Mrs. Brown or Cammy Jo know that she had arranged for them to be sent.

At the restaurant on Monday night, Mr. Brown had assured Kaye that even though the family would be moving to Lexington as soon as the school year ended, he would make sure that Cammy Jo was available for all the events of the wedding. There was something so controlling about the man that seemed to be hiding under the surface of his very quiet confident manner; it made Kaye's skin crawl. She just could not quite figure out why she was feeling like that. Maybe it was the picture Mrs. Brown had presented to her of the treatment she had received while living in their very nice, expensive home. Kaye wished she could understand Mrs. Brown's feelings.

Kaye took Cammy Jo and her mother back to the school and the two brothers came and picked them up. Cammy Jo waved goodbye and got into the back seat with her mother. The two brothers acknowledged Kaye with a nod of their head and drove from the parking lot.

The last week of school came with a flurry of activity. Testing was finished. Field day took place with the children participating in a number of outdoor activities. Everyone was under the direction of Mrs. Snyder, the P.E. teacher, who always pulled this day off with grandeur.

The grounds were covered with cars. This appeared to be the biggest crowd-drawing event of the year. Kaye was amazed at the number of people present and wondered how the lunchroom was able to make enough sandwiches to let all these people eat lunch. It was a great day, not too hot, but parents were slathering on the sunscreen to prevent a night of sleeplessness with a child burned to a crisp after spending the day out in the sun.

Most of the teachers took their students inside to enjoy a brown paper bag lunch, but Kaye was able to find a tree outside that provided enough shade so that her class could sit under it and enjoy the outdoors while they devoured their lunches. She made a big deal about picking up and disposing of all trash, saying, "Let's keep it green, kids."

Cammy Jo smiled up at her and said, "Miss Mason, did you know dat a kid is a baby doat? Are you calling us doats? Day smell weel bad." Cammy Jo had not overcome all of her speech impediment problems even with the best attempts of the speech pathologist, but she had improved.

"Yes, I know that a kid is a baby goat, Cammy. Have you ever seen a baby goat?" Kaye smiled back in responding to the child.

"One of the peoble on ouwere woad has some. They are weally cute."

"Yes, they are and that may be why little human people get called kids. Do you think it could be because little children are so cute?"

"Oh, so you tink we are cute and dat's why you call us kids and kiddos, Miss Mason?" Cammy Jo asked.

"Could be, Cammy Jo. I really do think my students are cute and much, much more than cute. They seem to get smarter everyday, too."

Cammy Jo seemed satisfied with this and scampered off to find Cory. The day ended with the last of the events completed, ribbons given out, and children finally loaded on buses or turned over to parents to make their way home. The teachers were more than ready to exit the building. It was time to get home and put up their feet and relax after a very exhausting day.

The last day of school arrived with Kaye wondering whether to cry or to be relieved. She was sad to see her students spending their last day with her as their teacher, but knew she had the rest of the month bursting with busy things to do for her wedding.

Cammy Jo had her dress to take with her to Lexington and Kaye had informed both sets of parents of the dates and times their students needed to appear. Cory would be picking up his little tux the day before the wedding. It was not a problem for his family as they lived right there in Hope Springs where the shop was located. The rest of the class was informed to be at the wedding a little early so Grandma Katie could make sure each one had a bottle of bubbles. Katie was just hoping the bottles would stay unopened until after the wedding. She had visions of bubbles floating around all during the ceremony. *Maybe,* she thought, *I should make sure I hand those bottles to the parents. That might solve the problem.* She tucked that thought away so she could use it on the day of the wedding.

The wedding went off better than Kaye could ever imagine that it could. But what Kaye liked most was the vows that she and Tom had written.

> I promise to be sharing the years with you-
> Everyday in everyway-
> So you'll never have any fears
> Through the glad times and the tears.
> Sharing the years
> When I am old and turning grey-
> Every day in every way-
> Know I'll always be your devoted wife
> As long as I can cling to life.
> Sharing the years with you
> So you can always love your life.

Tom repeated the same lines, only changing wife to husband. It didn't rhyme as well as Kaye's but they both loved what they had worked hard to compose together.

The reception was just perfect. The couple that owned the Tollhouse Restaurant had the new room ready and the caterer had everything prepared to perfection. The cake was absolutely beautiful and Tom even had time to enjoy his slice of hummingbird cake. It did end up being the bottom layer due to it being the heaviest layer of the cake.

Using the students made the wedding become an extra special, memorable event. During the reception, several of the children tried dancing with their parents and some attempted to dance with each other at the reception. Kaye knew the video of the wedding would be one she would treasure for the rest of her life, watching them blow bubbles and dancing with the stiffest legs as they tried to waltz with each other.

When the Macarena was played, however, they had learned to do that dance in the dance unit that Mrs. Snyder, their P.E. teacher, had taught. So everyone else cleared the dance floor when that song began and stood on the sidelines. Everyone was watching and laughing while her eight-and nine- year-old students never missed a beat and really enjoyed outperforming the adults.

Kaye found it really hard to say goodbye to Cammy Jo after the ceremony. She was holding back tears. She didn't want to cause any grief to surface that Cammy Jo might be harboring about having to leave all her friends behind because of having to move to Lexington. Cory's mom assured Kaye that she would be responsible for returning Cory's tux to the rental shop. The videographer got a good shot of all the students leaving at one time and waving goodbye to Kaye.

The best surprise came when everyone had left and Grandma Katie brought Kaye a suitcase packed with clothes for the honeymoon. "I think you'll find everything you need in here, Kaye."

"Why, grandma, I already packed my suitcase for the honeymoon."

"Yes, and it is on the back of Tom's truck. But you will need the things in here, too."

"The back of Tom's truck? I thought we were going to use my car and spend a few days in the Smokies and just travel around with no where in particular planned."

"Don't think so. Tom has been planning this for some time for you. I will let him tell you. He asked me to get this ready for you and I was happy to do it." Katie handed the suitcase to Kaye.

Tom appeared and Kaye looked at him with all kinds of questions in her eyes. He looked at the suitcase, smiled and said, "It's full of riding clothes. Some of yours and some new ones your grandmother was kind enough to purchase for me. I'm sorry, but I am not very good at selecting women's clothing yet." Kaye did not speak, but continued to look at Tom waiting for the rest of the explanation. "I have booked us a few days at a dude ranch out in Wyoming. We have a long drive ahead of us, but I have made overnight accommodations along the way. We will not be driving straight through. We do not have to hurry. We are not due there for three days. So we can take our time going out there. They have rides and cattle drives. We can attend campfires at night, go with the activities they have planned, or just enjoy the territory, or whatever else we decide we want to do. We are not committed to a schedule. I made sure of that before I booked."

"I can't believe you did this," Kaye said, somewhat taken aback.

"I do hope you are happy about it. You mentioned some time ago that you would love to take a vacation on a dude ranch and this one is supposed to be one of the best." Tom was beginning to need reassurance that he had chosen the right spot to honeymoon.

"Happy? It's perfect! Wisk me away, cowboy!" So Tom did just that. They changed out of their wedding clothes and headed west in comfortable jeans and cowboy boots.

Chapter 23

There were so many things to talk about and to discuss on the way to Wyoming. Kaye hoped that down through the years, they would always be engaged in the sharing of many interesting conversations. She had seen a lot of older people who barely spoke to each other. It was like they had run out of things to say. She wanted to be like her Grandma Katie and Grandpa Roth--always busy and discussing the day's events with each other.

Tom and Kaye laughed about some of the funny gifts the teachers gave her at her lingerie bridal shower that they held one afternoon before school was out. Grandma Katie and her mother had sponsored a shower too, using the church basement as the place to meet. That shower had been a little tamer than the one at school, but Julie Mayhugh had slipped in a real cute nighty and Kaye had packed it as a surprise for Tom.

Mark had offered to host a bachelor party for Tom. He even offered to hunt up some moonshine for the occasion. Tom had declined. He had recently watched a show on television about moonshining and one actor had described drinking moonshine: "You might as well set the glass on fire and swallow it." Tom wholeheartedly agreed with that description and saw no reason to put himself through suffering from a hangover after burning his throat out. It seemed like a double punishment in the name of fun. Didn't make sense to him. He and Kaye had a good laugh about that.

They discussed having children and how many they wanted. Neither one really knew or cared. They did know they wanted to wait a couple of years before trying.

Tom wanted to know what Kaye would do with the rest of her summer with no wedding to plan and no kids to teach. Kaye admitted that she had not really given that a lot of thought. She had just wanted to spend it with him. He reminded her that once they returned home, he would have a lot of catch up work to do there on the farm and the rest of the summer would require long hours away from the house.

"Since you love horses so well, why don't you help Mark out at his barn? You could get in your riding time and maybe help him to offer that youth riding camp for the elementary age children. I know he didn't find another horse at Tattersalls for you to share with the teenage girl, but you still have Stoney to show and you have to admit, Stoney is a lot of fun to ride."

"Yes, he is fun. I guess I could work there, if you don't mind, Tom."

"I don't. Mark is a pretty up-and-up guy. Besides, he seems fairly interested in Jennifer Lancaster right now, and I really don't think I have to worry much anymore about him luring you away from me."

"I'll ask him if he's still interested in doing the camp when we get back, and it would take an awful lot for anyone to be able to lure me away from you."

"I sure hope so. Kaye, you know how Lancaster sponsored Jason for the middle school camp? What if we sponsored Cody? I kind of grew to like the little guy during all those wedding rehearsals. He was a real well-behaved champ."

"I think that would be wonderful--if you want to do it."

"Great! We're on. It's getting dark and I'm tired of driving. The motel I reserved is just a few miles ahead. What say we get something to eat and claim our room?"

"I'm all for it." Kaye spent the first night of her married life in the arms of the man she hoped to be sharing the years with for the remainder of her life. It was pure bliss.

The dude ranch turned out to be more than the brochure described. The folks attending to the guests were more than gracious. The riding trails took the rider into breath-taking vistas. Plus, the dining hall afforded Kaye and Tom a chance to meet some really nice people who were also enjoying a dude ranch vacation.

Then there was the food, which was beyond wonderful. Kaye wondered how they were able to supply the items they did living so remotely in cattle country as they did. A delivery truck loaded with food showed up a few days later and that answered part of Kaye's question. The cook also showed Kaye a garden with new plants emerging, explaining that the kitchen staff spent a lot of time canning, freezing, and preserving their own food that was produced right there on the ranch. Kaye made a point to help Grandma Katie can this summer. She wanted food for her house that tasted this good.

The newlyweds almost didn't want to leave and return home. They had enjoyed everything about this honeymoon and the little cabin that had given them all the privacy they needed.

Katie answered the phone to find Chris Wilshire on the other end. She was not pleased to hear his voice but was polite enough to listen.

"Mrs. Mason, if you would, please, could you get a message to Kaye?"

"Why would I want to do that, Mr. Wilshire?" Chris noted that Katie had deliberately used his last name, even though when he had been at their house dating Kaye, her grandmother had addressed him by his first name. He knew this conversation was not going to be an easy one.

"Mrs. Mason, a client of mine, a Mr. Brown, is attempting to find his wife and children. His daughter was a student of Kaye's and he would like to know if Kaye has had any contact with them. He claims Kaye was very attached to his daughter."

"Which student was this?"

"Her name is Cammy Jo Brown." Katie froze, knowing that Kaye would not receive the news well that Cammy Jo might be missing.

"I will deliver the message to her, Mr. Wilshire. Would you give me phone numbers, please, so that if she wants to, Kaye can get in touch with you?"

"Of course, I will give you mine and Mr. Brown's in case Kaye does not want to talk to me."

"That might be wise, Mr. Wilshire. I will contact Kaye. I will not, of course, promise that she will get in touch with you."

"That's all I am asking, Mrs. Mason." Chris gave Katie the phone numbers and then said, "Thank you and goodbye."

Katie didn't bother saying goodbye. Roth yelled from the other room, "Who was on the phone?"

"You won't believe me when I tell you."

"Try me," Roth countered.

"It was Chris Wilshire."

"You're shitting me, Katie. What did that fool want?" Katie told him and Roth vetoed calling Kaye on her honeymoon to respond to an old boyfriend's request to call him. Roth didn't care if it did concern a missing child. He just didn't think it was wise. Besides, Kaye and Tom would not know anything about the missing child. They were returning home from half way across the country. Roth concluded the conversation with, "They are supposed to be home tomorrow and it can wait until then."

Kaye and Tom arrived home around midday the next day and Kaye called her parents and grandparents to report that they had made it back safely. Kaye said they would be over to see Roth and Katie later, so Katie decided to wait until that visit to tell Kaye about Chris Wilshire's phone call.

When she told Kaye, she made sure Tom was present. She didn't want Tom to think the family had the kind of family members who would keep secrets from him. Tom looked at Kaye and asked, "Wonder what is going on? Why would they be missing and how could that happen? You better call Chris, Kaye. I wouldn't want anyone thinking you were a party to that kid being missing."

"Oh, Tom, how could I be? I was on a honeymoon with you. If I need an alibi, I'll be calling on you."

"Okay, honey, do you want me to give them descriptions of how you spent your time?" Roth overheard that and suggested that maybe Tom should call and give Chris a detailed account.

"You two stop! This could actually be serious. Mrs. Brown did not want to go back to her husband. I know some things about the situation. Maybe more than I care to know and I can tell you that she just may have taken the kids and flown again. That is if she could get enough money and the means of transportation to do it." Kaye tried to explain without going into too much detail.

"Okay, Kaye, make the call," Tom instructed, handing her the phone. Kaye made the call and put it on speakerphone so everyone could hear.

"Chris, this is Kaye Scott," she said and smiled at Tom. He covered his mouth to smother a laugh and Katie and Roth just shook their heads trying to keep from laughing, too. They knew Kaye had used her new last name to irritate Chris and found it funny, but Katie shook her finger at Kaye all the same for being so devious. "What is up with Cammy Jo? Why is she missing?"

"Her mother has apparently left with her and the other child. I'm not sure I blame her. It appears that Mr. Brown is a bit more than controlling. He's the brother of one of our partners and I was given the assignment to represent him. It wasn't a job that I really wanted. You know how these divorce things go, Kaye. You can't really tell who is at fault or for what. Anyway, Brown explained to me that he always kept the keys to the cars and only gave them to his wife when she needed the car for some kind of domestic errand. I can't imagine that, but I guess that's the way his family life works. Apparently, Mrs. Brown had a key made one day when she was out in the car and also emptied a bank account with several thousand dollars in it before leaving. She had used the car the day before they all disappeared and had handed the keys back to Mr. Brown when she had come home. He had that set of keys to the car in his pocket when he discovered she was gone. I guess it never occurred to him that she could have a key made while she was using the car to go shopping."

Kaye was on the verge of laughing, but also on the verge of crying at the same time. If this lady got away, she was more than sure that she had seen the last of Cammy Jo. In a way, Kaye hoped the lady's escape would be successful. It sounded as if even Chris had discovered that Mr. Brown was a bit of a control freak.

"What do you want from me, Chris? I don't see how any of this concerns me."

"It really doesn't. Mr. Brown asked if I could get in contact with you. He thought I might have more information on where you lived than he did. You know you don't have a permanent address. You were living with your grandparents. He doesn't know them or how to get in touch with you, so I said I would try to call you. Have you seen or heard from Mrs. Brown or the children? That's really all I wanted to ask you."

"No, I haven't. Why would I?"

"Mr. Brown thought you were very close to his daughter. He said she was in your wedding as a flower girl and that you might know something."

"He is grasping at straws, Chris. I have been on a honeymoon for the past two weeks. Just got back today and I will assure you I was not helping Mrs. Brown escape while I was honeymooning."

"No, I suppose not. Hope you enjoyed the honeymoon."

"I did, Chris. I more than enjoyed it. Tom planned the whole thing and we went to a dude ranch in Wyoming and had a wonderful time."

"I'm glad to hear it, Kaye,"

"And, oh, by the way, I do have a permanent address now. I plan on being there for a very long time."

"I hope you are, Kaye. I wish you the best of luck and tell Tom that I said he is a very lucky man. Thanks for returning my call."

Kaye hung up, turned to the others in the room, and fell upon dead silence for a few moments. No one really knew what to say. Then Kaye burst out laughing. Everyone really looked surprised. "I hope the bank account she cleaned out was enough to keep her going for a while." The rest of the group couldn't believe their ears. This was so unlike Kaye. Then Kaye explained about Mr. Brown not letting his wife take her clothes with her when she left and went to live with the two guys in the hollow. She also told them about the other controlling habits he had and that Mrs. Brown felt her children were happier and freer living in that awful place in the hollow than they had been in the very expensive house that her husband was able to provide. It had become an expensive prison for the lady. Then Kaye added, "This time I hope she took plenty of clothes with her," and Kaye continued to laugh, even though nothing about the situation was really funny. She knew that even though Mrs. Brown was free for the moment, she had to be scared, and Kaye also wondered how long she would stay free. Kaye wiped away some tears and said, "I guess I will never see Cammy Jo again." Tom just held her for a few seconds and then said, "Well, in time, we can make a Cammy Jo of our own. What do you say to that?"

The next morning's paper carried a story about members of a family named Brown being missing and their car being found not too far from their home. The paper stated that no foul play seemed to be involved, but a large sum of money was missing from the family's bank accounts. The children and Mrs. Brown seemed to have just disappeared. There were no clues about where they might be or what might have happened to them.

Kaye cut out the article and put it away. She knew it was time to get on with her new life and that she could do nothing to assist Cammy Jo any longer. She just hoped that her teaching years were not filled with any more children that she would get attached to like Cammy Jo. It was too hard to let them go. Luckily for Kaye, she did have many, many more students that she really enjoyed and took a lot of pride in knowing and teaching, but there would never be another child that would have the affect on her that Cammy Jo did.

The following day, Tom asked if Kaye had called Mark. He stated that he thought she might be able to get her mind off losing Cammy Jo if she got busy organizing the youth riding camp. Kaye called Mark and found he was delighted with the idea. He told her he had a lot of older kids who could help her and asked if Katie would be helping, too. Kaye told Mark she would check with her grandparents and see what kind of help they would be willing to offer.

Kaye met with a group of young people from Mark's barn the next day that were willing to assist with the horse camp. She and Katie started organizing the events for the camp. They researched the Internet and found all kinds of things they were able to use in the camp. These activities had to be ones appropriate for younger children.

There were plenty of ideas readily available. The kids labeled and colored the parts of the horse on paper. They were able to watch when the farrier visited and learned about hoof care. Mark bought some small ponies that could be used with the smaller children. That move proved to be profitable when several of the children from the camp continued to take lessons after the camp came to a close.

A discussion took place about having a horse club at the different schools once the new school year began. All the older children helping Kaye with the camp wanted to be a part of the middle school group. A teacher was found at the middle school to form a club there. Kaye took on the role of organizer for Hope Springs Elementary Equine Club.

The Kentucky State Fair took place soon after school began and Kaye organized a fieldtrip to the state fair for all the camp children and Equine Club members. Tickets were purchased for everyone to attend the World Championship Horse Show on Saturday night. The school system allowed a bus to be used to transport students to Louisville for the event.

Many of the teachers went along on the trip, along with most of the parents of the children in the group. The night proved to be a great one with Jennifer Lancaster competing in the Pleasure

Class and winning it. She had a great cheering section as she made her victory pass.

One of Katie's Morning Moms had purchased a horse and had taken ribbons in a driving class earlier in the week. Katie had been there to see her show and was very proud to see her receive her third place ribbon. Roth had brought Katie to Louisville and they had spent a couple of nights, did some touring around Louisville, enjoyed the fair and attended a number of the horse shows while they were there.

One delight was seeing Michael show Secret under harness that week. Katie was delighted to see the young man take second place. They had shared the horse all summer and Katie had more than enjoyed showing Secret at the smaller shows during the show season. She, however, did not want the pressure of showing during the World Championship. It was just a delight to sit and watch the beauty of the American Saddlebred horses, the peacocks of the show ring, as they were called, make their way around the arena.

Roth had particularly enjoyed the show season. He was able to assist Miguel with a lot of the preparation for getting ready to go to the smaller shows, as well as give a hand at the shows, making sure every rider was safe by always checking saddle and bridle before giving a leg up to the rider. What he had enjoyed most, however, was watching Katie drive Secret. He knew she was in seventh heaven, and not only that, she was good. She had brought home several blue ribbons. He thought she had to be the prettiest thing he had ever seen flying around those arenas in that buggy. There were women much younger competing, but they just didn't outshine his Katie. She would be beautiful to him right up to the day she died. He wondered about eternity and hoped it would be possible to reunite there. He would be looking forward to it.

October rolled around with a big party at the barn to celebrate Halloween. The horses and riders were dressed in costumes with prizes given for every kind of entry that Katie and Kaye could think of, so that each horse and rider received some kind of award. Horse awards were apples, while awards going to the kids consisted of bags of candy.

The children put a lot of thought into the costumes. One rider dressed in Mexican regalia--complete with sombrero--had one of the small lesson ponies wrapped in strips of tissue paper so the poor little guy resembled a piñata. They were the 'Most Adorable' entry. Princess was really tolerant of Michael as he dressed as the Headless Horseman. One had to wonder what the poor horse thought of someone riding her who appeared to have no head. Michael took the award for the 'Scariest' entry. Another rider painted the bones of a horse on a black lesson horse named Licorice. The rider dressed in a skeleton outfit and was awarded the prize for the entry that was 'Hardest To Do'.

Cory and Jason teamed with another young boy who was riding at the stables to form the Three Musketeers. Kaye and Katie had to dig for a category for awarding those three with a prize, and finally settled on the entry 'Most Like a Classic Novel'.

The barn was making money and people were enjoying every minute of it. Jennifer Lancaster was getting more and more involved and offered to help organize some winter tournaments that could be held in Mark's barn. Mark was really pleased. It seemed that he was building a real family around the activities at his barn.

The show season ended with the Academy Nationals being held in Murfreesboro, Tennessee in early November. Several of the children who had attended the camps that Mark had sponsored in the spring and summer, and who had continued to take lessons, competed in the classes. The result was that Mark's barn brought home an enormous number of ribbons. Mark insisted that the ribbons be displayed outside the stall of the horse that was ridden to win the ribbon for at least two weeks. Afterward, the students were allowed to take the ribbons home as keepsakes.

Roth smiled when he thought about the young man named Mark Elliott who had appeared at his door over a year ago to see if Roth would let him rent his horse barn. The young man was well on his way to having a thriving business and Roth was very pleased that he and his family had been a part of helping him along the way. He had always tried to instill in his family a sense of caring and helping. But it appeared to him that Mark had helped the family as much as they had helped him. Katie was thriving working at the barn, and Kaye had kids thriving under her direction with beginning horseback riding lessons. When they moved on up to Mark, they really had cause to be confident and proud. He knew horses imparted a lot to a human being, but human beings with the right attitude could do a lot for each other, too.

Chapter 24

Fifteen years later

Katie sat on her front porch looking across the pasture fields that she and Roth had tended during the many years they were married. She smiled when she thought of Bill and Bob when they were young boys wrestling on the front lawn, with her yelling, "You all stop that! You're going to hurt each other."

The boys had not enjoyed the hard working tasks that farm life demanded and had moved away after college to careers of their own. But they always came back to the farm to celebrate holidays and for short visits while they were out there making a living for their families.

She was a little surprised when Bill and Jean had moved back and built a small house there on the farm. But she wasn't totally surprised. After all, Kaye and Tom were close by and that let the entire family enjoy seeing the daughter they had produced grow up.

Kaye and Tom had settled on the name of Tammy Jo for their child. That was about as close as Kaye wanted to get to the name of the child she had the first year she taught who had disappeared with her mother. Kaye had never heard from her again. Katie knew Cammy Jo had been very special to Kaye because she had never seen or heard her express as much concern over any other child she had taught as she had with Cammy Jo, and this was Kaye's sixteenth year to teach.

Maybe you become a little hardened to it all with more years of experience in teaching, Katie thought. But one thing none of them was hardened to was Tammy Jo. She seemed to be able to melt anyone's heart with just a smile. The child had been such a joy to all of them. Roth was gone now but had lived long enough with his damaged heart to see Tammy Jo show the filly he had raised called Homespun Honey. They had done quite well with that horse. Before she was turned over to Tammy Jo, Kaye had helped to break and show her. Once again Mark's skills in training were more than evident when Kaye showed her at Louisville in the Amateur Three-Gaited Class and won. It was one of the thrills of Roth's life and Kaye was floating with elation that night.

Kaye and Tom had tried to produce another child without success. After the delivery of Tammy Jo, the doctors were doubtful that Kaye would be able to conceive another child, and if she did, they doubted that she would be able to carry the child to full term. So, adoption agencies were being consulted and there was a child on the way that Kaye and Tom were expecting to receive. It was a boy and the nursery had already been redecorated from pink to blue for the occasion. Tammy Jo was ten now and was excited about the prospect of a baby brother.

Bob visited often and Bobby and Roxie had presented Bob with three grandchildren. A set of twin boys and a girl who Katie hoped would survive the antics of the twin brothers. Those twins gave Bill and Bob a run for their money when it came to rough housing. Bob had never remarried after his wife died. Many women had been interested, but he told his mother that he really had trouble filling his arms with another woman. He said he had been more than lucky once and would not be willing to risk a second marriage. He seemed content, so Katie had never encouraged him to find another partner. She knew she would not be out looking for anyone since her Roth had died.

She had received several invitations for dinner from some of the single men that were her age in the community, but it never seemed the same as when she was with Roth. She usually found herself digging for things to talk about with these men, and eventually, had not accepted any more invitations.

She had kept busy down through the years. Roth had built her that craft room that she dreamed about. It was where she spent many of the hours of her day. She did not spend a lot of time at Mark's barn anymore. Her age prevented her from doing that. She wasn't able to move quite as fast as she had back in her sixties and early seventies when she first started giving driving lessons there. She feared that, if something went wrong and a horse got out of hand for some reason, that she wouldn't be able to get out of the way fast enough. So, since she no longer mended as well as she used to, she decided that it was her turn to watch rather than to participate. She thought she had earned that right.

With Tom and Bill's help on the farm, Katie and Roth had been able to truly enjoy the last few years they had together. They had done some traveling and Roth had still been able to advise and help some with the tasks on the farm. He was active right up to the night he died when his heart just gave out. At age eighty-five, his passing was no big surprise, but all the same, unexpected when it happened. Dying in your sleep was something that Katie prayed for. Roth had done that and looked every bit at peace when Katie awoke the next morning. She remembered how heavy his arm felt draped over her waist when she opened her eyes. He had died with her in his arms. It was a memory Katie cherished.

Katie was finishing out her years with many wonderfully stored memories. She was surrounded by a family of love, and that was what Roth had always hoped would be the greatest achievement of the Mason family. It had been worth sharing the years.

Notes from Linda

This book is filled with many memories of horses that have been a part of my life and a part of the lives of many others. There was a horse, a mare, named Secret who lived with me a number of years and taught several young ladies to ride. She was a joy and a pleasure to me and gave us a foal named Princess who was also a beautiful spotted Saddlebred.

Memories of the roar of the crowd at Freedom Hall during the Kentucky State Fair World Championship Horse Show and the glory of watching the magnificent horses known as American Saddlebreds, along with watching the girls Secret taught to ride compete in shows like the one held at Murfreesboro, Tennessee, are items in my mind that I will always want to keep there.

The great and beautiful Kentucky countryside will always be a part of my life and memories. I would hope that everyone would have the chance to experience it.

On the following page is the Apple Dumpling recipe, which is referenced in the book. It appeared in our electrical co-op magazine, *Kentucky Living*, several years ago and I have used it time and again with success. I hope you enjoy it.

Apple Dumplings

2 cans crescent rolls (16 count)
4 apples (Granny Smith)
2 sticks butter
2 cups sugar
1 (12 oz) can Mountain Dew
          (or other clear soft drink. I use Diet Sprite to save
          calories.)

Grease a 9" x 13" pan. Unroll dough. Peel, divide apples into quarters, and seed them. (Optional: lightly dust apples with cinnamon.) Wrap each apple quarter with dough of one crescent roll, completely enclosing apple. Arrange in pan. Melt butter, add sugar, and bring to boil, stirring constantly. Pour over dumplings. Then pour the Mountain Dew over dumplings. Bake at 350 degrees for 45 minutes. Let sit 10 minutes before serving. Great with ice cream.

Submitted by Lillian Kazee
Salyersville
Kentucky Living Magazine, October 2009

Notes from Linda

Linda is a retired educator who spent thirty years helping children develop their writing skills. After retiring, she decided to take her turn at developing her own writing skills. Digging up a manuscript that she started writing over forty years ago proved to be a lot of fun and work, but her first published book, Shared Years, went live on May 31, 2013. Her readers have encouraged and are waiting for the release of the sequel, Sharing the Years. Proofreaders have reported the sequel is better than the first novel. Linda certainly hopes you agree. In her spare time Linda enjoys riding horses and a variety of activities including theatre, painting, music, and gourd crafting. She also enjoys riding in and driving the Model A Fords that she and her husband own. J. E. and Linda have recently purchased a home in Florida and are looking forward to spending time there as well as in their Kentucky home.